GLIMPSES OF GLORY

GLIMPSES OF GLORY

The Mowbray Lent Book 2017

DAVID BRYANT

BLOOMSBURY

LONDON · OXFORD · NEW YORK · NEW DELHI · SYDNEY

Bloomsbury Continuum
An imprint of Bloomsbury Publishing Plc

50 Bedford Square
London
WC1B 3DP
UK

1385 Broadway
New York
NY 10018
USA

www.bloomsbury.com

Bloomsbury, Continuum and the Diana logo are trademarks of
Bloomsbury Publishing Plc

First published 2016

© David Bryant, 2016

British Library Cataloguing-in-Publication Data
A catalogue record for this book is available from the British Library.

ISBN: PB: 978-1-4729-3428-4
       ePDF: 978-1-4729-3426-0
       ePub: 978-1-4729-3429-1

2 4 6 8 10 9 7 5 3 1

Printed and bound in Great Britain by CPI Group (UK) Ltd,
Croydon CR0 4YY

MIX
Paper from
responsible sources
FSC® C020471

To find out more about our authors and books visit www.bloomsbury.com
Here you will find extracts, author interviews, details of forthcoming
events and the option to sign up for our newsletters.

CONTENTS

CONTENTS

CONTENTS

PREFACE

I have written this book following a diagnosis of terminal cancer. As I look back over the years, various themes have stood out as milestones on my spiritual journey, and I have given them a (sometimes radical) theological slant. Biblical verses have often triggered my thinking. It is not my intention to convert the reader to a specific set of thought-forms, but I hope that it will encourage spiritual exploration and discovery.

The content has emerged from my experiences as a parish priest, a hospital chaplain, a one-time Samaritan, secondary school teacher and visitor to a top-security prison. Incorporated into the text are poetry and literature, those blessed gifts that have the potential to awaken us to an awareness of the Holy One. I make no apology for the non-orthodox nature of some chapters. We can only progress through questioning, questing and reflecting on the nature of God.

Nor do I claim to know the truth. I have simply outlined my journey of 78 years and shown how it has inexorably, if somewhat erratically, drawn me into the divine milieu. What has become clear to me, as the years have slipped by, is that the pathway to faith is not one of certainty but is a road leading to unknowing. God lies beyond human comprehension.

* * *

The book can be used as a basis for a Lenten study group or it can be read reflectively in private. I have intentionally dealt with the great themes of existence in random order, because life is always unpredictable and full of surprises.

The underlying theme running throughout is an unshakeable belief in the God who infuses every part of the universe, imbuing it with love. I have tried to show how glimpses of God's glory have shone out in the most harrowing circumstances, as well as in moments of joy and laughter.

Like the poet Gerard Manley Hopkins, my rock in this unstable life is a belief that 'the world is charged with the grandeur of God'.

1

Chaos

Genesis 1.2
In the beginning

The world is rife with uncertainty, which is built into existence and flows like a stream through the vagaries of life. Unlike our ancestors, we no longer live with belief in an ordered universe run by a God who instilled into it unalterable laws. Quantum physics has shown that particles behave in an indeterminate way. Astronomy has thrown up the barely conceivable idea that time alters its nature at the mouth of black holes.

Human experience serves to underline the apparent randomness of events, and the difficulties around prediction. Weather forecasting is a notoriously inexact science. Doctors often cannot foresee the progress of disease, and are reluctant to put a time limit on terminal illness. Brain surgeons do not know with certainty if a patient will emerge from a coma; and the national lottery illustrates the fickle nature of tossed, numbered balls.

Worse is to come. Not only is the future an unknown, but the past is irrevocable and the present no more than a fleeting moment, gone even as it arrives. We are carried along like helpless pawns on the inexorable conveyor belt of time. Philosophy has jumped onto the bandwagon of uncertainty via existentialism, and the belief that we have to formulate our own moral codes and try to stamp purpose on an irrational, meaningless universe. Small wonder that many turn to drink, drugs and other escapist devices, such as sexual licence, rampant materialism, the lust for power and the accumulation of possessions. The world of indeterminacy is truly a frightening and unsettling homeland.

Two events in the early 1960s brought home to me the enigmatic, puzzling thrust of life and the fear, distress and feeling of helplessness that is its spin-off. The Cuban Missile Crisis was a thirteen-day confrontation between America and the Soviet Union which came about as a result of Cuba's request to Nikita Khrushchev (then President of the USSR) to deploy nuclear missiles in Cuba. Fear, almost palpable, swept the country. Horrific memories of the nuclear bombing of Hiroshima and Nagasaki surfaced. Doom-laden newspaper headlines prevailed. This was a terror that could not be shrugged off like a nightmare; and throughout it all the nuclear clock ticked slowly towards midnight and Armageddon.

The tenor of life at my theological college changed. Personal prayer and liturgical services became imbued with a new intensity. Laughter died from the corridors of the hostel, and there was awed talk of extinction, death and radiation – subjects not normally broached by students. As we filed into chapel on 28 October 1962, the day the crisis was resolved, the air danced with our prayers of thanksgiving. We had been spared.

Two months later I found myself a young curate, naive, unsure and nervous. The summons came one night at two o'clock. A family that I regularly visited – granny, sick mother and a daughter of ten – had suffered a tragedy. The mother had died, and the grandmother could not face the task of telling the child. Would I come round and break the news when she woke?

I felt cold, and a blast of inadequacy swept though me. My experience of death and my pastoral expertise were virtually non-existent. How would I cope? What in the name of God could I say?

The pre-dawn hours ticked by in an agony of suspense. When she woke at 7.30, I held her hand, broke the news and gave them all a blessing; we said the Lord's Prayer through our tears. Life seemed very cruel, empty and bereft of hope.

As I said Evensong with my training vicar that night, the Old Testament reading was from Genesis: 'And the Spirit of God moved upon the face of the waters.' My whole being thrilled to the words; I knew that here was a watershed, and a life-changing concept. The destructive world of the Cuban crisis and the bedroom of the little girl were not dark, bereft and unrelentingly depressing. There was a redemptive factor in both: God, the Holy One, brooded over the chaos. In the words of the hymn-writer, chaos and darkness had heard God's almighty word and taken flight.

Transforming comfort swept though me, and it has remained every year, every day, since that time. Like Gerard Manley Hopkins, I believe with the depths of my being that 'The world is charged with the grandeur of God./It will flame out, like shining from shook foil.'

Believe that, and bow before the brooding Spirit. Then fear will drain away, and a blessed restfulness comes.

God the Holy One brooding over the chaos
of our lives, grant us a glimpse of your glory.
Amen.

2

Ladders

Genesis 28.10–13
Jacob's Ladder

Brute materialism is a comfortless stance. Deny that there is a spiritual element in the cosmos and a bleak picture emerges. Few have expressed this philosophy as starkly as Friedrich Nietzsche. For him, 'God is dead', and religion is a neurosis, an epidemic filled with a wealth of nonsense and superstition.

This is a harsh rebuttal of Christianity, and it implies that we are an isolated planet whirling in dark space and doomed to final destruction. Not only that, but we are forced, as a result of blind chance, to live in this inhospitable universe where, as Jean-Paul Sartre says, 'there is no purpose to existence, only nothingness'.

To live in such aridity requires more than a teaspoonful of Paul Tillich's 'courage to be', and a great deal of self-sufficiency; I could not do it. So is that it? Is life a nihilistic endurance test, a tortured journey through a cosmic desolation? If so, we might as well jump off the nearest cliff.

There is a way out of this impasse, and it comes in the unlikely shape of a ladder. As Jacob journeys towards Haran, he stops at sunset and lies down, using a stone as pillow. To wonder why he did not gather a handful of spinifex or desert grass is to miss the point. In those early Biblical days, animism – a belief that spirits dwelt in inanimate objects – vied with monotheism, a trust in one God. Travellers would make camp at sacred wells, trees, streams and rocks, in order to pacify the indwelling spirits and to call on their help. To place your head on a sacred stone was to be in communion with the holy. The stone held all the mystery of an altar or shrine.

With striking imagery the narrator illustrates this belief. No sooner has Jacob fallen asleep than he dreams of a ladder. Its foot touches the earth, and the topmost rungs reach to heaven. Angels descend and ascend, a pictorial representation of the reciprocal communication between man and God that lies at the heart of prayer.

The theological spin-off from this drama thrusts materialism aside and opens the way to a world where the sacred lies a mere hair's breadth away. This turns the Christian pilgrimage into a search for those unexpected ladders that link the sacred and secular, offering us respite from the godless, lonely world of Nietzsche.

Ladders of this sort appear as rafts in a stormy sea, lifting us out of despair and filling the world with joy. Search hard enough, and the humdrum sweep of existence shimmers with sublime moments when life with all its exigencies breaks through the barriers of the earthly into something altogether richer and profounder, redolent of the divine realm that lies within and beyond the world.

I discovered a ladder in hospital during the small hours of night in the high-dependency ward. In the neighbouring bed lay a young farmhand, in pain from a major operation, weeping for his lost health, desolate in a strange world of medicines, humming machines and disturbed nights. A trainee night nurse came to his bed and spoke words of comfort that I could hear though the drawn curtains. Human compassion opened a ladder to heaven, and I knew that God's presence was there in that corner of the ward.

The trigger for these holy moments is varied. It may be the smile of a grandchild or the peace in the lined face of an elderly nun. Climb Ben Nevis, and wonder with the Psalmist as he considered the natural world, the work of God's fingers. Ladders may materialize in the support of a friend, during the offering of the Eucharist or at the baggage carousel at the airport, when a fellow traveller offers a helping hand with the luggage.

For Yevgeny Yevtushenko, the Russian poet, it was love that transformed his days. He tells of how his whole existence was filled with elation when his lover's face appeared over his crumpled life:

> Then its particular light
> on woods, on rivers, on the sea,
> became my beginning in the coloured world
> in which I had not yet had my beginning.

Lent is a time for throwing back the bedclothes with a frisson of excitement, wondering what revelations of the Holy One lie ahead. It is like a sacred treasure hunt – in the words of Francis Thompson, 'Turn but a stone and start a wing'.

Take up the challenge, if you will, and use this season to search for ladders in our intricate, beautiful, sometimes hurtful world. Climb then rung by rung, and you may reach that point where the light of God turns the mundane into a glimpse of Paradise.

Lord, when despair blankets our vision and clouds hide our joy, let us hold on to your immeasurable love. Amen.

3

Towers

Genesis 11.1–9
The Tower of Babel

If ladders offer a pathway to heaven, towers exemplify the crushing pride of humankind. Written into our being is the desire to unlock the secrets of the universe and to unravel all that is hidden. The people of Babel decide on the ultimate feat of exploration, and attempt to build a tower reaching up to God. This, they claim, will give them everlasting fame. They gather a stack of baked bricks, mix bitumen for mortar and embark on their mission . . .

The project implodes into disaster. God turns their language into an incomprehensible babel, so that confusion and misunderstanding reign, and then scatters them to the four winds. The tower, derelict, stands as a pathetic monument to human arrogance.

All pride is an absurdity, for it dies with us in the grave. The poet Shelley illustrates the futility of vainglory. In the British Museum he observes the remnants of a statue of Rameses II, the once great Egyptian king. His vision expands and takes him to the scorching heat and wind-torn deserts of Egypt, where two vast, trunkless, stone legs, sightless and abandoned, lie half buried in a sea of sand, 'and on the pedestal, these words appear: My name is Ozymandias, King of Kings; Look on my Works, ye Mighty, and despair! Nothing beside remains . . .' That certainly knocks human pride for six.

In his novel *The Spire*, William Golding gives pride a religious spin, throwing it into a different dimension and bringing God into the equation. Golding's protagonist, Dean Jocelin, is obsessed with building a spire on top of the medieval cathedral. He refers to it as 'God's folly'. The harsh truth is different: the dean is living out his own arrogance and will to power; the spire is to be his memorial, his eternal claim to fame. Against all advice he insists on building ever higher. The result is ominous and doomed.

He is shown the sea of mud on which the foundations of the cathedral rest, and he hears the stone pillars singing under the strain. Nothing cracks his stubbornness. His reckless pride unleashes a flood of evil. A human sacrifice is buried in the foundations to appease the pagan gods, and the master builder turns to drink and attempts suicide. Dean

Jocelin himself contracts an illness that distorts him with a pain that racks him apart as he slowly subsides into madness. On his deathbed he looks out on the unfinished spire. All his proud desires have been swept away in a devastating finale.

Arrogance is insidious, and it has an underhand way of creeping into spirituality. Jesus repeatedly castigates the Pharisees for praying in public and giving alms openly. When the mother of James and John asks Jesus to grant her sons pride of place in heaven, she is given an uncompromising reply: 'You do not know what you are asking.'

Pride has many guises. It may appear as an urge for power, in the desire to be noticed and admired that prevails in our media-driven society. As the psychologist Jung said, 'Where love rules there is no will to power, and where power predominates love is lacking.'

Pride is present when we confuse truth with opinion. Dogmatic statements such as 'The Bible is true' or 'God answers my prayers' need unpacking: we are not stating ultimate truths here, but venturing opinions. To suggest that we are sages with divine wisdom at our fingertips is the antithesis of spirituality.

Another unattractive facet of pride is exclusiveness. To claim that the only road to salvation is through Christ is dismissive of a vast number of the human race. The disastrous legacy of religious intolerance is the world family being torn apart. Torture, death and homelessness are its brood.

When the pricklings of pride flutter into my mind, I recall the story of the young Trappist novice, in that strictest of the strict contemplative monastic orders. He was asked, 'What is prayer?' His answer has become central to my thinking. 'I don't know.'

The fourteenth-century writer of the anonymous spiritual classic *The Cloud of Unknowing* was equally modest. For him, God's mystery was impenetrable, his being hidden behind a cloud of darkness. All we can do is to 'strike hard at that thick cloud of unknowing with a sharp dart of longing love. And whatever happens, don't give up.'

The towers of self-righteousness, certainty and pride point ultimately to disillusionment and disappointment. They are ephemeral and futile. Rest in the cloud of God's love, and the divine hand, outstretched, will not fail.

Shatter the towers of our pride, Lord,
and let our rock in life be your reassuring
presence. Amen.

4

Names

Exodus 3.13–14
I am that I am

Even the name of God is sacrosanct, never to be disclosed. When Moses asks God to reveal his name, the reply is a brusque, quasi-philosophical 'I am that I am', a conundrum that leaves us in the dark. The reason for this divine reticence is that Moses is on dangerous ground: a name is a kind of shorthand that embodies all that we are. It gives us shape and personality, and proclaims that we are an integral part of the universe, and that we matter. Our name affords us a place in society, and gives us status. In asking the name of God, Moses is presuming an equality with him, a familiarity that demotes the greatness of the divine being. God lives beyond and above all names.

Not so for us. For humans, names are life-giving; without them we sink and waste away. I can still remember the National Service number I was given in 1955. It is an indication of how indelible are the depersonalizing mechanisms used by institutions to control their members. The kickback from this can be savage, as Kafka knew. In his novel *The Castle* he sketches the plight of a land surveyor who is never named but is referred to as 'K'. As K attempts to approach the castle, he is harried by malevolent, unseen forces. Confused and defeated, feeling insignificant, he is tossed around like a pawn in a cruel world.

More distressing still is the plight of Argentina's 'nameless ones', who disappeared when the military junta took over in 1976. James MacMillan's musical tribute to these unfortunates, and Ariel Dorfman's accompanying words, make the blood run cold: 'What did you say? They found another one? . . . Another one floating in the river?' The victim is naked and has been tortured beyond recognition, so that even his mother does not recognize him. As far as society is concerned, he has ceased to exist. Anonymity has obliterated him.

If we shrug our shoulders and think that that isn't our problem, there is something else that is. Our society is swimming with isolating terminology, whereby grouping takes precedence over naming. We assign people to separate, labelled drawers:

black, white, gay, straight, Muslim, Christian. Street beggars, alcoholics and drug addicts are notoriously anonymous. We rarely know their names, and they rarely register as we walk the streets. The dust of our lack of interest covers them like a shroud.

The more we exclude individuals from society, the more bigoted and judgemental society becomes. In this loveless climate, gang warfare, football rioting, street mugging, shoplifting and domestic violence thrive like rank weeds. There is an urgent need to re-personalize our towns, villages and housing estates, and that can only be done by standing fast against the tide of anonymity and facelessness that threatens to engulf the country.

Our world needs a massive injection of respect, love, recognition, appreciation and sympathy. The options open to us are stark: pass by and look the other way, or stop and tend to the wounded like the Good Samaritan.

One winter's night, trudging through the snow in my parish, I saw a light burning in a deserted barn. Inside was a young man, crouched over a fire of scrap wood. Raggedly clothed, unshaven, gaunt and filthy, he was the primal outcast. I asked his name in order to establish an empathy between us, and slowly his story came out. He was a heroin addict from one of the northern towns, trying to kick the habit. He had found the empty barn and saw it as a hideaway from temptation and the drug-sellers. He was wanted by the police for theft.

The parish provided him with new clothes and shoes from church funds, and found him a room in a hostel. He served his sentence of community service working in the churchyard.

Six months later, a transformed man, he called at the vicarage and presented me with a battered icon that he had found in a junk shop. It hangs on my study wall to this day. He had been given a name, and his being had flowered. It is salutary to remember, as we go about our daily business, that the street-sweeper may be a recovering alcoholic. The girl on the supermarket check-out is perhaps carrying an unwanted baby. The beggar with his cardboard sign has a mother and sister, and the old man pushing his pathetic belongings in a pram doubtless lives in loneliness.

Only God in all his glory remains nameless and infinitely compassionate. Those of us thrown into the turbulent stockpot of society need recognition and respect, for we are all in the same cosmological boat together, and none of us wants to go nameless to the grave.

*Lord, may we learn to uncover the hidden
glory in others so that we see your face
reflected in them. Amen.*

5

Tragedy

2 Samuel 18.33
David's lament over Absalom

The tragedy of the nameless merges into the universal grief of mankind embodied in King David's lament for his son. Despite Absalom's treachery, David's heart is in concert with all parents, and he desperately wishes that it had been he who had died, rather than his beloved child. The words resonate with pain and loss: 'Oh my son Absalom, my son, my son Absalom, Would I had died instead of you.'

Can any sorrow be deeper than that engendered by the loss of a young person? I doubt it. Those occasions in the past when I had to bury a child are built into my memory with searing clarity.

'Would you like to see her, Father?' were the mother's opening words. Her daughter lay in an open coffin in the parlour, as was then the custom in the West Country. Dressed in white, fair hair brushed, a bunch of freesias in her hand, she looked beautiful. For the parents it was an unbearable loss. As a young curate, I was stunned by the enormity of the human tragedy. How do we begin to cope with such grief?

One way is to throw the pain forward out of the unendurable present, in the hope that it will be lessened with the promise of an idyllic future. Poets, painters and musicians have given aesthetic expression to the premise of a future life. Victorian hymn-writers were adept at it. As wartime Sunday-school children, we frequently sang the sugar-coated words 'There's a friend for little children, / Above the bright blue sky'.

But there is a difficulty built into this prediction that strips the gilt from it. Its fulfilment involves the griever in literally a lifetime of waiting for reunion with their loved ones. All delay is physically and mentally draining; it has a cruelly eroding effect on the quality of life. It becomes 'something to be got through', a prison sentence that can only end with death.

Then again, the concept of life after death does not ring universally true. Parish visiting has brought me face to face with many parishioners, both atheists and churchgoers, who doubt it, or are at least uncertain.

So where do we go from here? Back to the past, and here there is a modest footing to be gained. To reflect on the ten glorious years of the child's life can bring into being the first fumbling steps of acceptance and an awareness that not all has been lost in the devastation. The child's life is written indelibly into the web and weave of creation, and in this sense has a permanency that time cannot destroy. To turn the pages of photograph albums and to relive the past with its joys, celebrations, excitements and laughter can sometimes bring a touch of wholeness and healing to broken hearts.

But we cannot live in the past for ever: that is spiritual imprisonment. So we must turn to the present, the Now, for that is the only locus in which we can rediscover the optimistic, ongoing force of life which alone can alleviate our grief.

One of the emergent evolutionists of the last century described the forward thrust of life as a bursting star shell. At the moment of its death, the firework gives birth to a thousand brilliant stars as a salute to the future and a promise of things to come.

Seen in this light, a few crumbs of comfort can creep in. There is something powerful and positive in the hurting response of the mourners and in the courage with which the parents try to restructure their damaged lives. In a strange way, the dead child has become the catalyst for what is uplifting and hope-filled. Out of the seething cauldron of human woes, from the cross of fire, something enduring and compassionate has emerged.

There is a passage in *Jane Eyre* that shows how even the soul-wrenching death of a child becomes a magnet for love. Jane's friend Helen Burns is dying of fever in the school infirmary. During the night Jane creeps into her bed and holds her tight. Jane whispers, 'Shall I see you again Helen, when I die?' The answer is whispered back, 'You will come to the same region of happiness, be received by the same mighty, universal Parent, no doubt dear Jane.' In the morning the matron finds Jane asleep, still holding the dead Helen in her arms.

When the world falls apart and we are broken and can see no hope, no future, love remains. For threaded into all the darkness and pain is God. That is my comfort and my hope.

Lord, when the darkness is everywhere and almost beyond bearing, come to us in your mercy. Amen.

6

Lust

2 Samuel 11.1–5
David and Bathsheba

Only too soon David's lament turns into lust, and his dalliance with Bathsheba. My reflections on this misuse of human sexuality sprang from an unlikely source. Years ago, a young couple were somewhat self-consciously sitting in my study asking about holy matrimony. 'We've been living together, I'm afraid, Vicar.' The lovers had breached what they thought was the ecclesiastical establishment's code of acceptable behaviour, and they expected castigation. After all, wasn't the church against sex? My reply startled them. 'Good. Then maybe you have experienced something of the God-given heights of sexual pleasure, and touched on the depths of human love. It will be an unsurpassable start to your marriage.'

My response to the bride-to-be and her partner was not intended to be frivolous. I wanted to set straight the church's dismal record on sexual morality, and to make it clear that desire and love are gifts, not curses.

The root of the church's prudish anti-sexualism lies in the scriptural dualism that rips apart spirit and body, elevating the first to mystical heights and writing off the body as tainted. This theme runs through the Bible from beginning to end. Adam and Eve in the creation myth do not delight in their bodies but cover them with fig leaves in shame and disgust.

Then there is St Paul's curmudgeonly approach to the sexual: 'It is better to marry than to burn.' He piles on the disapproval still further, claiming that the *sine qua non* of being a follower of Christ is that we crucify the flesh with its passions and desires. It seems to me like self-harm. That, coupled with his tirades against women temptresses, is a damning indictment indeed: 'If a woman will not veil herself she should cut off her hair.'

It gets worse with the doctrine of original sin – that outrageous belief that we are born sinful. As the psalmist mistakenly says, 'Behold I was brought forth in iniquity and in sin hath my mother conceived me.' The conclusion to be drawn is that sexual craving and physical pleasure are the arch-sins that will strike us down.

I am not an advocate of unbridled sexual licence, a throwback to the libertine 1960s. Of course not: that would lead to moral anarchy, as it did with King David and Bathsheba. David, walking on the roof of his palace, saw Bathsheba semi-clothed, bathing. Lust kicked in, and he wanted her at all costs. He hatched a plan whereby Uriah, her husband, was sent to the forefront of the battle, where he was killed. David's self-centred indulgence had a mal-evolent outcome: murder.

This leads to a caution. Sexual activity that involves degradation, violence, coercion, deceit or abuse has to be thrown out of the Christian window. The whole thrust of Christ's teaching on morality underlines that. But what of sexual encounters that fall outside those parameters?

Focus for a moment on *Lady Chatterley's Lover*, D. H. Lawrence's much-maligned novel, which was finally published in an unexpurgated version by Penguin in 1960. Prior to that it could only be bought from a dingy bookstall underneath the arches of Waterloo Station, complete with brown paper bag.

Those who disgustedly panned the book had it wrong. The lurid descriptive scenes where game-keeper Mellors and Lady Chatterley have sexual intercourse may be in bad taste, but there is nothing in them to condemn. In themselves, they were morally neutral, neither right nor depraved. What is morally questionable is Lady Chatterley taking advantage of and deceiving her crippled husband, and Lord Chatterley's failure to meet his wife's emotional needs. In other words, it is the attendant circumstances that give any sexual act an ethical overtone.

Sexuality is not something to be sniggered at, as it was in the case of Lawrence's book. Nor should it be entombed in archaic laws drawn up from isolated verses plucked out of the Bible. Remember, St Paul was expressing his own views, not those of a loving God. Even less should sexuality be reluctantly tolerated as a pandering to human weakness. To hijack sexual encounter and turn it into a gender argument about who should sleep with whom is to distort it.

Sex is a unique blessing, a source of deep fulfilment, a profound joy. It is there to be reciprocated and appreciated. But there is one overriding condition: if it is done in the name of Christ, it must not be hurtful or destructive.

With that one proviso, to accept the divine gift of sexuality with anything other than gratitude and delight is churlish. It cocks a snook at God, the giver of all good things. Not only that: human sexual encounter, when infused with love, is a reflection of the unbounded love of God. That is why the young couple in my study had my blessing.

Lord, may the delights of human sexuality bring us to an awareness of the infinite depths of your love. Amen.

7

Kindness

Jeremiah 38.7–13
Jeremiah is rescued from the well

God's love has many facets, and kindness is one of them. When it seeps from the divine realm into the human, the world smiles. The Old Testament tale of Ebed-Melech is a winner. The prophet Jeremiah is in deep water. He has been railing against the adultery, greed and slander that bedevil his society. This does not make him popular. When he prophesies doom, his rating falls to zero. He correctly predicts that soon the Jewish nation will be led in fetters to exile in Babylon. This is high treason, and King Zedekiah has him thrown into a dank, mud-filled cistern.

A good Samaritan appears out of nowhere in the shape of Ebed-Melech. He is a non-person in the eyes of the people: an Ethiopian, an alien and a eunuch. He approaches the king and begs him to release Jeremiah before he dies of hunger and thirst. He is taking a mammoth risk. Crossing the king usually meant a death sentence. Against all odds, the king agrees. Ropes and old clothes are lowered. Jeremiah puts them under his armpits to avoid chafing, and he is drawn up into the fresh air. That is true kindness.

Sometimes kindness and its scion, friendship, are deeply demanding. John Steinbeck's novella *Of Mice and Men* tells of two migrant field-workers in California during the Great Depression. George is intelligent but uneducated. His friend Lennie is a lumbering simpleton with great strength but little mental ability His one love is to stroke the soft fur on rabbits. The farmer's daughter-in-law, bored out of her mind, flirts with Lennie in the barn, and allows him to stroke her silky hair. Feeling his great strength, she panics and screams, and the terrified Lennie accidentally snaps her neck.

The two men become outlaws, and Lennie is the target for the vengeful crowd intent on hanging him. They camp that night, and George weaves a comforting tale in the smokey darkness as he lies beside Lennie. They hear the crash and shouts of the lynch mob as George, infinitely gentle, tells Lennie that soon they will buy their own farm and there will be rabbits for him to stroke.

The ending is horrific. George raises his gun and shoots his friend. 'He brought the muzzle of it close to the back of Lennie's head. The hand shook violently, but his face set and his hand steadied. He pulled the trigger. The crash of the shot rolled up the hills and rolled down again.' The inert body of Lennie jars once and then hunches forward into the sand where he lies without quivering. That is a real compendium of kindness, friendship and courage.

The media rarely present the public with kindness. The human catalogue of wrongdoing is, sadly, more likely to make the tills ring. Christ presents us with a diametrically opposed world paradigm of limitless kindness – an outgoing of concern that ropes in prostitutes, lepers, outcasts and the unlovable.

The world with its unfolding vista of experience offers us countless opportunities for showing kindness and friendship. I remember my first day at boarding school, aged nine. Abandoned on the grass outside the preparatory block, fearful of bullying, sick with the thought of impending loneliness, it was as if my world had dissolved. Wanting only to hide from the fear of it all, I found a ledge outside the junior boys' changing-room, took several marbles from the pocket of my grey, utility, wartime shorts and started to roll them along. Then a treble voice piped up. 'Can I play too?' It was another new boy, hair awry, eyes still wet from recent tears. It was the start of a lifelong friendship.

Kindness does not always involve a sacrifice as monumental as George made for Lennie, turning himself into a murderer. More often it is comprised of the slow, incessant drip of our often unnoticed concern for others that fires the world. Never under-estimate small acts of kindness: they urge forward the kingdom of God. What better driving force in life could we have than that of the psalmist: 'Surely goodness and mercy shall follow me all the days of my life'?

It would make a good epitaph on a gravestone too.

*Our every act of kindness flows out
into the sea of God's love, always enriching.
So help us to be generous-hearted,
Lord Christ. Amen.*

8

Suicide

Samuel 31.1–7
Saul falls on his sword

Suicide demands an outpouring of our kindness, for it springs from desperation. King Saul is approaching his Calvary. In disguise, he visits the Witch of Endor, and asks her to summon the Spirit of the dead Samuel. The oracle's words are chilling: 'Tomorrow you and your sons shall be with me. The Lord will give the army of Israel into the hand of the Philistines.'

The dreadful prophecy comes true, and the wounded Saul begs his armour-bearer to run him through. The man refuses to kill the Lord's anointed, so the king falls on his sword.

When I was thirteen, my mother drew up for us children a list of proscribed books, which of course we read surreptitiously under the blankets. One of them was Thomas Hardy's *Jude the Obscure*. She was trying to protect us from what must be one

of the grimmest depictions of suicide in all literature. Ill fortune follows Jude every step of the way.
His first marriage fails, and his longed-for place
at university never materialises. He ends up as a
stonemason.

He falls in love with Sue Brideshead, his cousin.
They have two children, but she refuses to marry
him. They take in Little Jude, the sickly child from
his first marriage, but the family are treated as
outcasts for living in sin. In this travesty of domestic bliss, the children feel rejected, unwanted.

Jude, ill, finds lodgings for himself, and Sue visits
him. He is watching the breakfast eggs boil when
she screams. All the children are hanging by the
neck behind the door. Little Jude has left a note:
'Done because we are too menny.'

There is no doubting the pain that seethes out
when somebody commits suicide. I saw many
instances of it during my ministry. There was a
farmer who hanged himself rather than face financial ruin. A parishioner came to me in tears. Her
brother had jumped off an oil derrick in the Middle
East. As a hospital chaplain I once visited a young
woman in a side-ward with red rope-burns scarring
her neck: her attempt had failed. Each left in its
wake a legacy of guilt, loss and profound sadness.

One incident has haunted me over the years. I was on a long-distance train, returning from Plymouth to Darlington. The train stopped at Exeter, and a party of young students clambered on. One of the girls glanced at my dog collar and made a bee-line for my seat. 'Can I talk to you, Reverend?'

It had all the hallmarks of a 'chat up the vicar' joke, and I was tired. But no. Three hours earlier her boyfriend, a long-term depressive, had intentionally taken a lethal dose of tablets in the bathroom. He could no longer face the pain of his existence, and she was travelling to her parents for comfort.

Her anguish flooded out. First came anger at a God who stands by idly while a young man destroys himself. What had she done to deserve this? Slowly her God-directed rage turned inwards. She was responsible. She had not been sympathetic enough. She had failed. Then the accusing finger turned to her dead lover. In upending the pill bottle, he had deserted her.

I listened, and said little, for the wound had to be drained. When her grief ebbed away, I encouraged her to talk about life with her boyfriend. She told me of agonized nights spent battling his depression. Interwoven were the joys of physical love and the memory of Greek holidays shared together.

I learned of his magic touch with watercolour and the thrill as they turned the key in the front door of their first flat. She talked, and wept, and wove her tale till journey's end.

I watched her walk away at Darlington feeling profoundly inadequate. I had done nothing to help her. She had done that herself by painting a picture of the man she loved, brushstroke by brushstroke. Nobody could take that away from her.

To claim that suicides are cowards is cutting and cruel. Their actions are a cry of despair so desolate that only oblivion can bring ease. The Christian ethic demands that we hold suicides and their relatives close to our hearts in prayer. If one comes into our family ambit, we can only weep and hold the hand of the one who has died. I guess Christ would have done the same.

*When pain overwhelms us and we cry in
the night-time, Lord, hold our hand in the
darkness. Amen.*

9

Laughter

Genesis 17.17 and 18.9–15
Abraham and Sara laugh

Just as the parched earth longs for winter rains, so our sometimes sad world needs the wellspring of laughter. Laughter is the music of the universe, heralding concord and warmth, allowing the world to flower and burgeon.

I love the story of Abraham and Sara chortling at the thought of a pregnancy when she is already one hundred years old, for Biblical humour is almost unknown. Jesus weeps but never laughs. The apocryphal gospels, which never made it into the canon of scripture, reverberate with laughter and eye-twinkling scenarios. The Virgin Mary, aged three, dances on the altar steps, encouraged by the grandfatherly priest holding her hand. The *Proto Evangelion* tells of a group of laughing children running away to hide when Jesus approaches. It is the primal game of hide and seek. When Jesus is thrashed by the crusty schoolmaster for getting stuck on the second letter of the Hebrew alphabet, he gives the academic an erudite rundown on the origins of the Hebrew alphabet. What a pity such hilarity has been excluded from the Sunday readings.

Religions – and spirituality, when it is starved of humour and shot through with self-importance and solemnity – are sour and moribund. They need an injection of holy laughter. This came home to me when I was a theological student, sub-deaconing at High Mass in St Cyprian's Clarence Gate, one of London's famous Anglo-Catholic churches. The ritual was performed faultlessly, and during the week we ardently studied the handbook *Ritual Notes*. Mistakes resulted in a dressing-down in the vestry from the vicar after the service.

One Sunday morning the church was ablaze with candles and misted with incense, and we three ministers, garbed in rich vestments, were about to cense the altar. The congregation waited, soundlessly engrossed in the mystery and sacredness. Just as we reached the south end of the altar, the celebrant slipped off the step and the three of us cascaded backwards, sending the credence table flying. Bread and wine and silver lay in an unholy muddle on the paved floor. The tight smile on the lips of the Master of Ceremonies spread like chicken-pox, and, try as we might to hold back our mirth, the entire sanctuary party was soon convulsed with laughter. Handkerchiefs dabbed at eyes; teeth were firmly clenched in a vain attempt to still the hilarity.

A muted rumble from the congregation revealed that they too had fallen to the contagion of laugh-ter. It was odd. Instead of feeling that an outrageous sacrilege had been committed and the liturgy mocked, the reverse was true. Our laughter seemed to eddy heavenwards, floating past the massed angels until it reached a benignly smiling God. Laughter had transmuted into prayer.

What is more, it gave birth to another theological side-shoot. We had drawn enjoyment, amusement and humour into the very heart of the sacrament, enriching and glorifying it.

But we have to be wary. Flip the coin of laugh-ter, and a darker side is revealed. Laughter can be destructive and cruel. The isolating laughter that accompanies teasing in the playground causes untold pain. The cynical laughter when those we dislike are in the mire is alien to Christianity. Laughter speckled with the derisory or humiliating is void. It is a symptom of spiritual sickness.

Laughter infused with Christ's love is holistic and revivifying. Go to the maternity ward, and the air is joyful with the laughter of thrilled parents and the chuckle of babies. Such laughter surely reaches to heaven. Listen to the secret whisperings and watch the smiles that drift across the faces of a young couple who are discovering a love that goes beyond mind, memory and measure. It is a blessed harmony in the often raucous music of the world. Just as precious are the mingled laughter and tears of a bereaved widow as you turn the pages of a photograph album with her, looking at pictures of her departed spouse. Smiling through her tears, she laughs with remembered joy as she says, 'Look at this one. It was Venice, and us on our honeymoon.'

Once I saw healing laughter in the terminal children's ward. The ten-year-old son of the woman who cleaned our church hall had a vicious virus and was dying. I tried to imagine the mother's pain. No words came to me. There were none adequate. Her distress had passed beyond that point.

Three days later we visited again, full of foreboding. He was playing football in the ward with another lad, using rolled-up pillowcases. 'It's a miracle,' said the Sister. We all laughed, a quiet song effervescing with joy, thankfulness and relief.

Laughter is one of our God-given building bricks. It can be used to humiliate, hurt and scoff. Conversely, it has the potential to lighten up the world and to transform darkness. What a responsibility and what a gift! Go your way and use it to God's glory.

Lord, may the music of love-filled laughter ring out across the universe, awakening us again to your presence. Amen.

10

Story-Telling

Daniel 3.1–30
Daniel is thrown into the furnace

All the appurtenances of a blockbuster film are here. King Nebuchadnezzar builds a towering, golden image of himself in the desert and assembles a discordant orchestra of horn, pipe, lyre, trigon, harp and bagpipe. He summons all the high and mighty of the land preparatory to demonstrating the most arrogant ego-trip in the Old Testament. When the cacophony reaches a climax, all are ordered to bow down and worship the power-hungry king. Daniel and his friend refuse: image-worshipping is not their spiritual scene. Their God is far superior to the ludicrous effigy of Nebuchadnezzar.

The king is furious, and threatens them with the furnace. They refuse a second time, and Nebuchadnezzar turns apoplectic, instructing the boiler man to heat the furnace seven times over.

Surprisingly, the furnace does not explode; but Nebuchadnezzar's arrogance does.

An angel leads the men out of the fire unharmed, and the belittled Nebuchadnezzar decides to throw his hand in with another psychotic announcement. From now on, anybody who refuses to worship Daniel's God will be ripped apart and their houses razed to the ground. I can just see my grandchildren enjoying a hotted-up version of that for their bedtime story.

This leads straight into historicity, and the question 'Is the story true?' If it is, it gives birth to a distorted conception of God. He becomes as bizarre, unpredictable and infantile as the gods of Mount Olympus. He hatches a plan, sanctions the throwing of men into a raging fire, tosses an angel into the mix and causes the laws of thermodynamics to halt in their tracks. If the story is swallowed whole, then God is playing silly games and is an image of Thomas Hardy's despicable 'President of the Immortals', who pulls the puppet-strings and makes Tess of the D'Urbervilles dance out a life of living hell.

There is no footage in making a historical claim for Biblical tales of this ilk. The story of Daniel needs to be viewed as a high-flown, rhetorical drama, eminently readable and – assuming that is all it is – good fun, from which we are invited to extract meaning.

There are myriad possibilities here. It could be read as a timely reminder of man's inhumanity to man. Perhaps it sets us off on a theological exploration of angels. For me it is a lively, pacey and colourful depiction of God's love, which never fails even when the furnace is heated seven times and life is inhospitable.

To struggle over the historicity of the Bible rather than seeking to unearth the meaning in its rich tapestry of poetry, psalmody, parables and ethics, alienates not only the atheist but also those who are hovering on the edge of belief. I guess it gives the person in the pew, not to mention the clergy, unease and a few darts of doubt.

Some years ago I was stopped in the street by a flummoxed dentist. He had attended a church service and heard the story of Peter walking on the water, which had left him fuming. As a scientist, he believed that the world operated in an ordered way and that miracles were nonsense. A story about somebody striding across a lake was ridiculous – a hotchpotch of make-believe – and he had no time for it.

He had a point. I could not credit it myself, and never had. It flew in the face of reason, as well as physics and chemistry.

But that was not the end of the story. It was possible to assimilate it another way. So I urged him to reorientate his perceptions and not to think in terms of historicity but to search for meaning. To debunk the historicity of a story does not necessarily detract from its value as a story. King Lear may not have been a real, reigning king, but the play still contains gems of truth about human behaviour.

So we re-envisaged the story of Peter over a pint of beer, so that it became a picture-language exemplification of God's abiding love. When we are at our wits' end, fearful and sinking beneath the weight of existence, a healing hand often appears metaphorically out of the darkness. Seen in this light, the story ceases to be nonsensical but evolves into a narrative that offers hope and reassurance to a needy world.

Six months later, the dentist joined the church choir.

To struggle with the historicity of the Bible or slavishly to accept its verses as ultimate truth is to stultify our spirituality and to insult reason. Search the miracles, parables, psalms and Biblical

utterances for meaning, and a new, exciting world
of ideas is thrown open. Go for it.

Lord, let us always be open to the freshness
and mystery of your written word, and free
us from thinking we can unravel your truth.
Amen.

11

Brutality

1 Samuel 15.33
Samuel Kills Agag

The Old Testament abounds in scenes of brutality. Armies are massacred, individuals are put to the sword, Abraham is all set to sacrifice his son, and Daniel and his friends are thrown into a furnace. Perhaps most gruesome of all is the scene where Samuel hacks Agag to pieces. Agag is king of the Amalekites, Samuel's sworn enemy, and to his shame Samuel kills him in the name of God. No Sunday lesson reader could end this passage with the familiar 'This is the word of the Lord.'

Brutality is not the preserve of the Old Testament. It is an abscess that poisons the world. For some regimes, torture has become standard practice, and the bombing of innocent civilians is passed off with a shrug as collateral damage. Our sick society thrives on it. Pick up a paperback thriller and more often than not it outlines the horrendous practices of a depraved serial killer. The television has a nine o'clock watershed, after which violence and cruelty have a free hand. Forbidden sites on the internet reputedly have pictures so degrading and dreadful that the thought of them makes you shudder.

Is there no let-up, not even a chink of light, to stem this unholy tide? George Orwell's book *Nineteen Eighty-Four* is a fearsome condemnation of the violence and cruelty inherent in a totalitarian state. It was turned into a film some years ago. The scenes with Winston Smith on the pain machine are enough to try the strongest stomach. He is a low-ranking member of the ruling party in the nation of Oceania, stationed in London. The secret thought police analyse his every move for signs of disloyalty. The party prohibits free-thinking, individuality, sex and love, and Winston lives in perpetual fear.

One day he receives a note from a dark-haired girl called Julia which reads, 'I love you.' Ominous feelings bubble up, and the reader can sense impending disaster. The relationship blossoms into a covert love affair, which is doomed from its outset.

Julia and Winston rent a room above an antique shop, not realizing that the owner is a spy for the thought police. They are betrayed, and Winston is horribly tortured in a building known as the Ministry of Love. He is thrown out onto the street, the party leaders confident that they have destroyed his love for Julia. Then comes the redeeming moment, shining out from the hopelessness. As Winston lies dying on the ground, he stretches out his hand and Julia's hand comes out to meet it. It is a great song of triumph, a blessed conclusion. The evil power of brutality has not won. The human spirit has soared above it, undefeated.

Some years ago, when we lived in London and our children were small, we paid a Chilean girl to look after them while we were at work. As time went by, she told us the gruelling story of her life under the brutal hand of General Pinochet. Her sister had been tortured for expressing left-wing sentiments.

After six months this girl decided to return to Chile and her family. We were devastated. Surely she would be put in prison, and become another victim of the regime. She was adamant. The risk had to be taken, for it was her homeland – despite the blanket of horror overshadowing it. She loved her family more than her own safety. So she went, and we have often wondered what happened to this brave young woman. She was a ray of light, a candle burning steadfastly in the blackness of the regime.

Turn to the passion of Christ and the same picture emerges. Jesus lived his last days surrounded by brutality. Nails, a crown of thorns, scourging and crucifixion are his lot, yet none of it destroys his compassion. Right at the end he commends his mother into the hands of John, the beloved disciple. On Golgotha, brutality confronted love and found it indestructible.

There is a temptation to sigh and shake our heads when we read of violence in the newspapers. We feel helpless, unable to lift a finger to stem the tide of cruelty. Despair blends with hopelessness. But we are not powerless. We can hold the situations clasped firmly in our compassionate prayers, strong in the belief that God's love is plaited into even the worst situations of our human making. That is a paradox, but it is one that can keep us from the abyss of total despair.

Lord, our acts of violence break the world apart. May we weave a tapestry of life that brings about wholeness and healing. Amen.

12

Holiness

Exodus 3.1–6
Moses and the burning bush

Too much pain and brutality blunts our senses, so it is not an indulgence now and then to shy away from the unbearable. Holiness is a good resting-place, a harmonious milieu in which we can find renewal and fresh endeavour. When the burning bush explodes into flame, God alerts Moses: 'Do not come near. Put off your shoes from your feet, for the place on which you are standing is holy ground.'

Only too often we kick holiness in the teeth. The tiny village church shimmered under the Andalucian sun, its walls gleaming whitewash. Here, surely, I would find a heaven-haven of peace and holiness.

Not so. A bevy of scantily clad tourists was encamped in front of the tabernacle chewing *bocadillos*, swigging lager from cans. This could be dismissed as no more than a display of insensitivity towards the local culture. On a deeper level, however, the carousing was symptomatic of an insidious malaise. Secularity had run rife here, and there was a defiant rejection of respect and a two-fingered salute to the spiritual.

'Holiness' is a word that too often conjures up images of stained-glass windows, sanctimonious faces, kneeling on cold stone floors and interminable prayers. But that is not holiness: it is piety.

Holiness is an awareness that there is more to the cosmos than meets the eye, and that there is an insoluble mystery at the universe's heart. The world is an enigma that science and philosophy cannot solve. That said, there is more to holiness than an awareness of the limitations of human intellect. Interwoven into it is what the theologian Rudolf Otto called *mysterium tremendum*: an awe-filled mystery that can leave us trembling at the sheer wonder of it all.

Peer through an astronomer's telescope at Jupiter's moons or the Orion nebula, witness the birth of a baby or view the Alhambra during a rose-coloured sunset, and you will instinctively know what this means.

All is not plain sailing. Like love, holiness cannot be learned as a textbook exercise; it can only be awakened, and the stimuli that bring this about are all around us. Wordsworth knew this.

> And I have felt
> A presence that disturbs me with the joy
> Of elevated thoughts; a sense sublime
> Of something far more deeply interfused,
> Whose dwelling is the light of setting suns.

Many experiences can kick-start this awareness. Sublime ancient monuments such as Stonehenge or the Pyramids can stir our sense of the numinous, the sacred. So can silence, half-light, music and drama. Sexual awakening and proximity to death too: all have the power to bring about heightened awareness.

Surely the world has a more potent weapon with which to forge the future and shape the present? I doubt it. Holiness recreates our perception of the environment. We no longer want to litter it with decaying nuclear material and poison it with landfills. Nor do we have the inclination to vandalize or destroy.

Transfer this conception of holiness to people, and the prospect is even rosier. Violence, abuse and hatred only sneak out from the woodpile when we view humanity with disrespect or disdain. Once you see the numinous in your neighbour you do not mug him or rape her. Holiness transforms our very being and enriches our spirituality.

The pursuit of the sacred was the driving force for many of the mystics and saints. Hildegard of Bingen was an aficionado of holiness. 'There is no creation that does not have a radiance, be it greenness or seed, blossom or beauty.' The world's numinosity left St Augustine stirred to the heart of his being. 'What is this which gleams through me and smites my heart without wounding it? I am both a-shudder and a-glow: a-shudder in so far as I am unlike it, a-glow in so far as I am like it.'

Some months ago I saw a bed of dahlias in a public garden. Their heads had been crudely ripped off and lay withering in the grass. That is the obverse of holiness: a desecration and violation. This summer I was shown a spotted crake – a bird that is very rarely seen – skulking in a reed bed. That once-in-a-lifetime sight thrilled me to the core. It was a glimpse of holiness. A pavement mugging is a destruction of the sacred. The smile on the face of a new mother as she cradles her baby is an expression of the *mysterium tremendum*.

The holy ground around the burning bush represents not just a few yards of parched, singed soil but the whole world. Search for the holy in nature and the sacred in people, and bow your head before it.

Dear God, the sacred permeates your creation. Open our eyes to the numinous that lies all around us. Amen.

13

Possessions

1 Kings 21.1–16
Naboth's vineyard

'Buy our shirts and be happy.' The poster stared me in the face as I waited in a traffic jam on London's Westway. The absurdity of the claim was self-evident. How could a garment comprising two sleeves, a collar and some pieces of cotton bring joy? The subtlety of advertising is that it creates a spurious sense of need and then offers to satisfy it. In short, we are being conned into thinking that we need material goods and that if we lack them we are inferior. The undesirable spin-offs may include a sense of inadequacy, restlessness, jealousy and dissatisfaction, which leads to crime, for example burglary.

The outcome for King Ahab and his wife Jezebel, with their unfettered greed, was terrible. Egged on by his wife, Ahab cooks up a false charge of treason and blasphemy and accuses Naboth. The crowd stone Naboth to death, and the triumphant king seizes his spoils. The much-desired vineyard is his at last.

But not for long. Retribution quickly follows. Ahab is struck by an arrow in battle, and Jezebel ends up being thrown from the palace windows and eaten by dogs.

Christ advocated a radical alternative to materialism and the acquisition of possessions in the form of an altruism gone mad: if somebody steals your coat, give him your shirt as well. In his novel *Les Misérables* (and famously depicted in the musical and the film inspired by the book), Victor Hugo tells a moving story depicting the emptiness of possessions. It concerns a Christ-like bishop who gives refuge to Jean Valjean, a freed galley slave. He offers the ragged visitor the best bedroom in the palace, and entertains him as lavishly as his simple means allow. In the morning, to the consternation of the household, a basket of silver has disappeared and Jean Valjean with it. Later that day the police return with the convict and the silver, which has been found in his possession. Valjean is petrified, knowing that his punishment will be a death sentence. The bishop turns to the gendarme and says, 'But I gave the silver to Jean.' Then he takes from the mantelpiece two silver candlesticks that have great sentimental value for him. 'And here are the candlesticks I gave you last night. You must have forgotten to take them with you.' When the police disappear, he says, 'Jean Valjean, my brother, you no longer belong to evil but to good. It is your soul that I buy from you. I withdraw it from black thoughts and the spirit of perdition and I give it to God.'

The bishop reminds me of the saintly Brother Lawrence, a seventeenth-century lay brother in a Carmelite monastery. The simplicity of his life is a dismissal of the world's goods. 'We can do little things for God. I turn the cake that is frying on the pan for love of Him. It is enough to pick up but a straw from the ground for the love of God.'

Simplicity often surpasses the transient pleasure of wealth. The Russian dissident and writer Alexander Solzhenitsyn found a moment's joy in snow. He had been imprisoned in one of Stalin's gulags; for exercise, he was let out into a tiny, high-walled yard. He bent down, picked up a handful of snow and ate it. It was, he said, the happiest day of his life.

I used to visit a mother who was paralysed from the waist down and could only lie on her stomach. She spoke by turning her head sideways on the pillow and looking up. She lived in a poorly furnished council house and was alone for most of the day. Her husband worked on the dust cart and often did not get home until six o'clock, as they needed the overtime.

Sometimes I would read aloud to her, for she could not manage a book by herself and novels drew her into a world away from her disability. I never heard her complain, and there was a serenity in her face, a look of peace that I have only previously seen in the wrinkled visage of an elderly nun.

I was present one day when her two young children came back from school. She welcomed them with an outstretched hand, a smile and kisses. She had found a contentment that many of us never discover in a lifetime.

Possessions do not make for happiness. Only love and an inner contentment can do that. Over the years that mother has been my constant mentor and teacher as I think of her lying helpless on the bed. I thank God for her short, blessed life.

Liberate us, Lord, from the bondage of possessions, for you alone are our treasure. Amen.

14

Rebuilding

Nehemiah 4.1–9

Rebuilding the walls of Jerusalem

I take my hat off to Nehemiah for his resilience and endeavour in the face of concerted hostility. He was a favoured cup-bearer to the king of Persia, living in Susa. Word came to him, no doubt via a camel train, that the walls of the city of Jerusalem had fallen into decay and disrepair. He asked the king for permission to make the long journey to his homeland in order to put reconstruction work in motion. The king furnished him with letters of authorization and ordered that he be given as much timber from the forest as he needed.

A desolate sight greeted him. Tumbled brick-work, missing mortar and shattered rock were everywhere. It was a mammoth task, made more difficult by his enemies. No sooner did he rebuild a section of wall than an overnight sortie of vandals would knock it down. The workmen were subjected to caustic remarks – 'A fox could knock over your flimsy structure . . .'

Undaunted, Nehemiah appointed guards and set up watchtowers, which were manned overnight. Against all the odds, he got the walls rebuilt and in good shape in a mere fifty-two days. Now that really was an achievement.

Rebuilding broken people, or helping those who have been knocked apart by life to restructure themselves, is far more difficult. I never cease to wonder at the courage with which the hurt and damaged draw themselves out of the mire. Irina Ratushinskaya, the Russian poet, was arrested on 17 September 1982 and charged with anti-Soviet agitation and propaganda. She was sentenced to seven years' hard labour in a strict-regime camp. Her crime was to have written poetry.

Conditions were dreadful in the small zone, a women's unit set aside for prisoners of conscience. She suffered beatings, force-feeding, brutal treatment from the wardens and the savage cold of Russian winters. For some weeks she was at death's door, but was nevertheless put on a bread-and-water diet in a freezing cell. She suffered concussion from persistent beatings on the head, and was often put in isolation in an unheated cell. Out of this hellish environment she wrote poems on scraps of paper and leaves, and they were smuggled out for the world to see. Her courage was supreme.

In one of her poems, written on a winter's night in solitary confinement, she tells how a sudden sense of joy and warmth would surround her and she felt wrapped in a blanket of love as she huddled by the icy wall.

Someone is thinking of me now,
Petitioning the Lord for me.
My dear ones, thank you all,
Who did not falter, who believed in us.

The world's prayers and her determined 'courage to be' kept her death at bay. In 1986, bound copies of her poems were given to President Reagan and Mikhail Gorbachev and she was released. Like Nehemiah, she would not give in and, like the phoenix, rose triumphant from the ashes of her past.

I met a woman in the parish whose courage in rebuilding her life has stayed with me over the years. She was in hospital with her one-year-old baby, terribly burned. She had set her house on fire in utter desperation, in order to escape from an unbearable marriage in which cruelty, depravity and

aberration prevailed. The first hospital visit I made
to her remains vivid to this day. Her features were
unrecognizable, and thick foam covered her face
and limbs where she had been burned. The child,
less seriously ill, was in a side-ward. Weeks, months
of painful skin grafts and operations followed,
and the ward sister told me it was doubtful that
the mother would survive. But she did, and the day
arrived when she asked me for a mirror to see her
ravaged, rebuilt face. I held her hand and prayed.
'I am ugly,' she whispered. 'Nobody will love me
now.' I answered in the words I knew by now to be
true: 'But you are beautiful within.'

She came home and, during the summer months,
walked with her pram in the vicarage garden, for
she did not want anybody to see her scarring. A
year later I saw her strolling along with the toddler,
arm in arm with a young man. Her ravaged face
was peaceful and touched with new happiness. She
had rebuilt her life, and I could feel the renewing,
healing love of God all around like mist.

I smiled and waved, and my lips formed the
words of the Gaelic blessing:

May the road rise to meet you.
May the wind be always at your back.

May the sun shine warm upon your face.
May the rains fall softly upon your fields and,
until we meet again,
May God hold you in the hollow of his hand.

Rebuild our broken lives, O God, and give
us the courage to be. Amen.

15

Passion

Song of Songs
Reflections of divine love

The Song of Songs is a paean, a hymn of praise to
sexual love. In unbounded erotic language it describes
the encounters of two lovers and their yearning for
each other. The imagery is rich and evocative. On
one occasion the woman remembers a visit from her
lover when the land was basking in the beauty of
springtime. She imagines him as a shepherd pastur-
ing his flock among the lilies. There is no hint of
chastity here, no coyness or modesty. The lover is
ravished by a single glance from his beloved, and she
invites him to enter the garden and taste the fruits.
The duo play out their love story to the accom-
paniment of a chorus represented by the daughters
of Jerusalem. The Song of Songs is a fable unravel-
ling the ecstatic love between God and his people.

At first it seems a curious medium for describ-
ing contemplative prayer and spirituality. But the

mystics frequently spoke of their intimacy with God, and their ultimate goal was spiritual marriage with the divine.

In his sublime poem 'Dark Night', St John of the Cross describes his journey to God as a deeply moving love affair that left him faint with desire and tenderness. On a dark, secret night he slips away unseen from his house as fire pounds in his heart. It is a journey of the soul. The very darkness of the night is transformed, so that it becomes friendly and cosseting. He finds the loved one who fondles and caresses him beneath the cedar trees. There, in that transport of delight, in the arms of God comes a peace and happiness that surpasses any other.

> I lay. Forgot my being,
> and on my love I leaned my face.
> All ceased. I left my being,
> leaving my cares to fade
> among the lilies far away.

One of the great love stories of our time is that of Dr Zhivago and Lara, his mistress. Zhivago and his wife and small son decide to escape from the revolution and tumult of twentieth-century Russian history and go to Varykino, the beautiful estate and house belonging to her grandfather. During the long winter months Zhivago travels by sled to Yuriatin and in the library sees Lara, a woman who has several times in the past fired his heart and imagination. A two-month-long love affair ensues before he is captured by the partisans and forced to work as a military doctor. He is freed two years later and returns to find Lara. His family have gone to the relative safety of Moscow. He and Lara set up home in the deserted house, which is covered in icicles, frosted with rain, its old-fashioned decadence showing a kind of beauty amongst the dust and cobwebs.

It is a doomed affair, for they are both on the authorities' black list. Zhivago persuades Lara to return to Moscow while he stays on at Varykino. He promises to join her shortly. Their parting has an intensity that wrenches at the heart. The scene in the film where Zhivago rushes to the top of the house to watch Lara's troika disappearing over a crest of snow is almost unbearable in its pathos. His words tell all. 'I love you wildly, insanely, infinitely.' This was truly a love beyond all knowing. 'They loved each other, not driven by necessity, by the blaze of passion often falsely ascribed to love. They loved each other because everything around them willed it, the trees and the clouds and the sky over their heads and the earth under their feet.'

There is another angle to this. All human love is a reflection of the love between God and humankind. A mother's love for her child, a father's caressing of his son and daughter's hair, is a flicker of divine love. A young couple in the heights of sexual ecstasy know something of this. So do doting grandparents and the elderly married whose once dynamic love has melded into care, compassion and gentleness. Teenagers engaging in the first fumblings of physical discovery and mental empathy are responding to the Holy One's love.

The German theologian Martin Buber sums up this marriage of divine and human love in words of great intensity. 'He who loves a woman and brings her life to present realization is able to look in the Thou of her eyes into a beam of the eternal Thou.' Pray God that we may all have a glimpse of his eternal love here on earth.

Lord, let our love grow and deepen so that it furthers your kingdom of light. Amen.

16

Mercy

Jonah 4.6–11
God refuses to destroy Nineveh

God instructs Jonah to go on a mission to Nineveh, proclaiming its imminent destruction because of its moral laxity. Fired by his importance, Jonah travels to the city only to find, to his disappointment, that the inhabitants have repented in sackcloth and ashes. He returns ill at ease, and begs God to carry out his plan of monumental destruction. God chides Jonah for his lack of mercy and refuses. As Jonah lies exhausted in the desert heat, God makes a plant grow up to shade him. It dies overnight, and Jonah pities it for its arid, untimely death. Then God chimes in. 'You pity the plant ... And should I not pity Nineveh.' So the town is saved, together with 'much cattle'.

There is another delightful Old Testament story that illustrates God's mercy. The people of Sodom are morally reprehensible, and God is on the point of eliminating the inhabitants. Abraham pleads for them. Will God restrain his hand if 50 righteous people are found? The bargaining goes on, Abraham knocks God down to ten men, and He agrees to stay his anger. It is a colourful and amusing tale, but it carries a weight of theological truth. God is not a destroyer, a cruel judge, vengeful, remote and intractable. His nature is compounded of mercy, forgiveness and love.

Mercy is one of humankind's more appealing traits. It usually comes about when somebody in power exercises kindness and consideration, rather than misusing their authority. I recall an incident from my schooldays. I had done well in the end-of-term Greek exam. The master summoned me: I was to move up into the top class next term. Fear hit me like a douche of cold water. The senior Classics master was a figure of fear. In those lawless days of the 1940s, beatings, clouts round the head, cruel words and physical punishments were commonplace. He was a tyrant, a misuser of power; in today's gentler climes he would be locked up for abuse.

The dreaded day came, and we were set a lengthy piece of Herodotus to study for our homework. It was way beyond my capabilities, and one of the other boys passed me an English translation of the passage. It was written in stilted, antiquated language of the sort that no schoolchild would ever use. My turn came, and in fear and trembling I read from the crib. Of course, he knew it was nestling under my desk. He knew too that I was bottom of the class, and struggling with Greek. So he exercised mercy, did not thrash me and passed on to the next desk with a grunted, 'Well done, boy.'

Our concepts of God often turn God's compassion upside down. We reduce God to a stern Freudian father figure and clothe him with derogatory words, maintaining that he is judgemental, stern, disapproving and even retributive. This terrible, skewed picture of God is found in the pages of Albert Camus's novel *The Plague*.

The town of Oran has been struck down with a lethal disease: bubonic plague. Fear builds to a climax as more citizens suffer and die. The young son of Monsieur Othon, a town magistrate, catches the plague and dies after a long and painful struggle. The Jesuit priest Father Paneloux preaches a sermon claiming that the plague is a punishment, a scourge sent by God because the citizens have turned their backs on him. Dr Rieux, the local physician, is outraged, as well he might be. 'No, Father. I've a very different idea of love and until my dying day I shall refuse to love a scheme of things in which children are put to torture.' It is a significant moment when the hard, unbending priest kneels at the bedside of Othon's son and begs his tyrannical God to let the child live.

I could not worship a God who lacked mercy. Prayer would be an empty charade if I thought God was an avenger, a dictator. Only a God who is absolute love is worthy of worship. I go along with St Francis, who saw creation as overflowing with divine mercy, compassion. 'Such love does the sky now pour down, that whenever I stand in a field I have to wring out the light when I get home.' That is the God for me.

Bless me with your forgiveness, Holy God,
and show me mercy. Amen.

17

Loneliness

Psalm 137
The exiled Jews hang up their harps

Psalm 137 is a lonely cry from the heart. As the exiled Jews think of their beloved homeland hundreds of miles away, they sit down by the waters of Babylon and weep. They hang up their harps on the trees, for who wants to make music in so disheartened a mood?

Loneliness lurks behind many a door, as I discovered from parish visiting. Humans are conceived, nurtured, educated and married each as a being apart from all others. That is the way things are. I am I, and you are you. Nothing can cross the divide, not even the closest companionship, the passionate kiss or sexual union. The well-tried old-timers of alcohol and drugs paper over the cracks of loneliness, but with morning comes a rude awakening to our isolation. To fill our days with activity may give us an uneasy illusion that we are not alone, and may provide a raft to grasp in rough times. Sadly it is a flawed procedure, because it addresses the symptoms of loneliness but does not remove the disease. Even in the midst of happy laughter and partying we can feel alone – perhaps even more so, because they contrast with the solitary days that we have to endure.

Loneliness is thought of as the affliction of the elderly, but it crosses all barriers of age and culture. I recall the very overweight girl who wept because her uncontrollable urge to eat left her un-partnered and friendless. Then there was the farmer whose remote farmstead I visited. I was the first priest he had seen in seventeen years. The loneliness of bereavement and loss is only too well known.

All is not lost. Toss the coin of loneliness and you discover that it has another face: aloneness, which is creative, renewing and spiritually energizing. Sometimes we thrive on it. The artist needs the emptiness of a studio before he can paint. The composer withdraws so that, uncluttered by noise and movement, he can produce a symphony. No novelist can write in the middle of Trafalgar Square.

There is a strange contradiction here. Each artist in his own way is alone, but in his aloneness he finds he is at one with a deeper reality which lies beyond and from which he draws his inspir ation. Indeed, part of his skill is to lure us into that other world until we lose our sense of isolation and find communion. Then what we feel is no longer anguish but peace. Look at the world of the Cape Horn yachtsman, the mountaineer, moorland walker or astronomer, peering out over empty vastness. They welcome the solitude. It is an old friend that subsumes them, and they find in it an affinity with the world, a sense of belonging.

George Mallory, the famous mountaineer who disappeared on the north-east ridge of Everest in 1924, said this on reaching a mountain crest: 'Is this the summit, crowning the day? How cool and quiet. We're not exultant but delighted, joyful, soberly astonished. We have achieved an ultimate satisfaction.' There is no hint of loneliness there, only the knowledge that aloneness can be inspiring and peace-filled.

The demons of loneliness certainly haunt us, and in our sense of separation they are formidable. The fear of illness, bereavement, depression and a sense of life's futility fuel the fires. But if, like Daniel, we beard the lions in their den, something remarkable happens. If we can find the courage to jump off the precarious foundation of papered-over cracks, we will discover that we are still upright. Instead of letting us plummet, the world has stretched out a helping hand. To give that a Christian spin, the uplifted hand of God never fails. If we recognize that, newly positive statements spark out like hammer blows on steel: 'Yes, I am alone, but not bereft. Yes, I can manage, because divine love encircles me.'

In his sermon on loneliness and solitude, the theologian Paul Tillich comes up with a profound truth. The spectre of loneliness is banished because of the presence of the eternal upon the crowded roads of the temporal. In other words, the face of Christ shines through everybody and everything in this world, including us. So we are bound together by that invisible bond. The Christian demand on us is to take that love to all who sit by the waters of Babylon weeping in their loneliness.

Be with us in our loneliness, Lord, and let
the shadow of your wings hover over us.
Amen.

18

Escape

Psalm 139
The omnipresence of God

I tried escaping from God for nine barren years. Disillusionment set in after a painful divorce that left me reeling. I turned my back on the church, for its platitudes and claims seemed empty and pointless. A teaching post in an inner-city London comprehensive kept me in pocket but led to immense stress and dissatisfaction. Weekends became a blur of alcohol and drugs, a blessed oblivion. I was in a milieu of profound emptiness and, like Sartre, could find no philosophy that was not ultimately futile and false.

I felt like Saul Kane in John Masefield's poem 'The Everlasting Mercy'. His descent into hell was vivid and violent. He bit his father's hand and broke his mother's heart in two. He fought his best friend unfairly for money, and one drunken debauch followed another. Finally, he lay in the hay with

Jane, the local doxy, 'And shut out Christ in husks and swine'. In a drunken frenzy he rushed naked from the inn and rang the village fire bell.

Inexorably he slides into a spiritual death, confronting the parson with damning words: 'I don't believe in Prayer or Bible./They're lies all through and you're a libel.' His alienation is final. Good has become evil, evil has become good, and he is in hell. He meets a Quaker woman in the inn and taunts her for being pious. Her words are redemptive.

> Every drop of drink accursed
> Makes Christ within you die of thirst.
> . . . every dirty word you say
> Is one more flint upon his way.

I pitied Saul Kane and I pitied myself. Self-loathing makes for an uneasy, hateful bedfellow.

In time I returned to the church, sought sacramental forgiveness, remarried, and slowly my spirituality emerged from its hibernation, just as it did for Saul Kane. He greets the new dawn and sees Old Callow ploughing. He has become a Christ figure, and for Kane the young green shoots in the field represent the Eucharistic bread: 'O Christ, the plough, O Christ, the laughter/Of holy white birds flying after.'

Psalm 139 takes up the song; it is my favourite in the entire psalter. It carries for me an incontrovertible message: God is omnipresent, infiltrating every moment of our life. 'Where shall I flee from your spirit?' the psalm writer asks wistfully. The answer is, nowhere. God is with us in heaven and in hell. He follows our flight to the uttermost parts of the sea. He is with us in the darkness, and night for him is as bright as the day.

St Augustine wrote a memorable prayer about escape from God. His early life was like that of Saul Kane. Eventually the day of reckoning came. 'I came to love you too late, Oh Beauty, so ancient and so new.' He railed like a madman against the beautiful things and beings that God had made, but once God had touched him he burned to have his peace.

I part company here with the materialism that soured my earlier days, for I believe now that we are comprised of body and soul. That is to say, there is a spiritual element within us, invisible to the surgeon's knife, beyond proof. To maintain that is to take a leap into the dark, and that I gladly do, for I have tried the world without such a creed and found it be empty and haunted. We are good at nourishing our physical bodies with exercise, moderation and visits to the doctor. But if the spiritual is neglected, thrown to the four winds or allowed to stultify, there is an inner distortion, a part of us that finds no fulfilment of peace. So an integral element of our being withers.

I have close friends who have no time for organized religion. Doubtless they would disagree with me here and call themselves atheistic, but their kindness, generosity, willingness to be on call at times of difficulty and their lifelong support when I was at my nadir are to me an exercising of that inner soul. Theirs is a sweet spirituality that has been my comfort for years.

St Clare of Assisi's words speak to me of the folly of seeking to flee from the Holy One. 'Place your mind before the mirror of eternity! Place your soul in the brilliance of Glory! Place your heart in the figure of the divine substance! And transform your whole being into the image of the Godhead itself.' Yes, and yes again.

When we are deep in the darkness, your presence holds us safe. Keep us from despair, Lord Christ. Amen.

19

Prison

Jeremiah 52.10–11
The imprisonment of Zedekiah

Zedekiah's terrible fate is mirrored in the misery, hopelessness and darkness that pervade top-security prisons today. It was a closed world to me until I joined New Bridge, a charity that arranges visits to prisoners who request them. I was given Home Office security clearance to visit Category A prisoners, and signed on.

So it was that I found myself in a queue outside one of northern England's most restrictive prisons one Saturday afternoon, trembling at what lay ahead. My visitee had committed two murders and a brutal rape. He would never be released.

Huddled against driving sleet, the line of waiting visitors looked like a pre-glasnost Soviet bread queue on a Moscow street in winter. Hatchet-faced men drew on cigarettes; women with empty, abandoned eyes stood sullen. We waited silently with British stoicism.

Entry procedures have a Kafkaesque quality that fills the would-be visitor with unease and dread. Visiting orders are scrutinized. Handbags, carriers and presents are confiscated, bodies searched. On we shuffle to the metal-detector. Prison is not for the claustrophobic. Ten consecutive sets of electronic doors have to be passed. They open and close in pairs, trapping you in a temporary limbo. For the final indignation hands are stamped with a mark visible only under ultraviolet light. Without it, you will not be released. It is to ensure that you are not an escaping prisoner masquerading as a visitor.

In the special visits room reserved for Category A men, prison officers stood guard against the walls. Absurd questions flutter into my mind. Why are institutional walls painted green? What if there is a riot and I am taken prisoner with a knife at my throat? One by one the men appear through an unmarked door, and there he is: insignificant, nervous and wary. Surrealism abounds. I am stirring sugar into my tea chatting about the traffic jam near the Metro Centre when suddenly the terrible nature of what he has done disorientates me and I wonder why I am there. I study his features, looking for signs of madness, the demonic. I cannot find them. He quizzes me eagerly about the world outside, and I ask a few intrusive questions about his. It holds a sickening fascination for me.

'Time up,' shouts the head officer. A pandemonium of misery breaks out. Desperate hugs are exchanged, seasoned lags exchange platitudes, women leave, shoulders bent in misery. There are no redeeming features here, no carefree laughter, only a cold, hard hostility that leaves the air heavy and ominous.

But I am wrong. In the waiting room I strike up a conversation with a young girl and tell her I am a priest. Her man killed a soldier in a drunken bar brawl. He had served nine years of his twelve-year sentence, and was shortly due for release. He had asked for forgiveness from God and for a blessing from the prison chaplain, bitterly regretting his crime. She had been disowned by her family.

'Do you still love him?' I ask. 'Yes, I won't give up on him. We are going to get married.' Suddenly the grim, sterile waiting room seems less sombre. Human love has penetrated even this cruel zone, and surely all love springs ultimately from God.

Then another flicker of light touched the scratched green walls. A young woman rushed in. Her train from Plymouth was delayed for an hour, and she had missed visiting time. She pleads for the authorities to make an exception. The laws remain unbreachable, draconian. She collapses into a chair, curled up like a foetus, weeping. An older woman, face lined by hardship, kneels down on the cold, stone floor and begins to stroke her hair in long comforting sweeps, murmuring quiet, unheard words of comfort. Then she holds the girl in a Christ-like embrace.

I cleared the last electronic gate and walked out into the fresh air. At that moment the sun broke out of a troubled sky touching the slate roof of the prison block, turning it mellow. I knew then that the love of God infused even this forsaken place, bringing with it the seeds of potential hope and redemption.

As I drove down the A1, past the rusted metal figure of the Angel of the North, a thin finger of peace woke in me. God and his holy ones encircled that hell on earth with its drab green walls, locked cells and legacy of wrongdoings too terrible to recount. It was a milestone for me. I had found God where I thought he could not be.

Transform those places where darkness rules, and let your light break in, O Christ. Amen.

20

Alienation

Ruth 1.15–22
Ruth and Naomi

The generous-hearted Ruth refused to abandon her mother-in-law, Naomi, and insisted on accompanying her to a foreign land. 'For where you go, I will go and where you lodge, I will lodge.' John Keats poetically describes her heartbreak. Maybe the nightingale's song that he is listening to 'found a path/Through the sad heart of Ruth, when, sick for home,/ She stood in tears amid the alien corn.'

We live in a society where alienation has become the norm in the streets of any large town. I recall, one afternoon, walking down the Marylebone Road with traffic streaming past in all directions. Half in the road and half on the pavement lay a meths drinker, insensitive to his predicament, with the churning wheels passing perilously close to his body. Nobody made a move to pull him to safety. He was a loser, a no-hoper, homeless, no more than an empty shell of a human being. So why bother?

Then there was the middle-aged *Big Issue* seller on the streets of a northern city, face turned to the wall, weeping. Crowds swarmed by, not seeing his need, or seeing it and preferring to pass by on the other side. Others showed faint curiosity. His world had fallen apart, and his lodging arrangements had collapsed. Nobody cared. Alienation is all around us.

Most sad are those occasions when it poisons inter-faith relationships. Surely those who try to follow a spiritual path should find harmony and peace together? But only too often we withdraw behind a barrier of dogma, doctrine, scripture, ethics and history that are the hallmarks of our particular religions. There the mood hardens. We become fearful of strangers, jealous of our own spiritual traditions and ruthless in our attempts to promulgate them.

With this deepening of the divide comes a growing polarization and the claim that our faith alone offers salvation, with the unspoken implication that all who differ are spiritually in error. As we sink deeper into our private kingdoms, intolerance turns to active hostility. Disciples of other faiths arc seen as a potential threat, hopelessly misguided and far from God. Finally the whole religious edifice crumbles into war, fanaticism, discord and violence. At that point the last, faint glimmer of holiness dies and only hatred remains.

Most people who believe in God take a less rigid stance when face to face with those of other faiths and opt for tolerance, at least in theory. We engage in cross-cultural dialogue and ensure that education is, as far as possible, all-embracing, not skewed towards one particular set of beliefs. We endeavour to establish a society that is broad enough to incorporate our different codes of dress, manners, customs and religious observances.

That is all very well as far as it goes, but tolerance is an undemanding virtue. It often means no more than relegating to the category of irrelevant, or faintly odd, the deeply held beliefs of others. So long as they do not encroach on our way of life, we are not overly concerned.

That is an uneasy truce. Something far more radical and painfully sacrificial is required. We need to engender a world of mutual, outward-going respect, a field of warmth that far surpasses mere tolerance. This demands a cleansing of our negative thought patterns so that we slough off all resentment, mistrust, prejudice and exclusivity, leaving the soul free for divine love to pour in. The compassion and acceptance generated by this soul-purging would enable us to understand that truth is elusive and imprecise, rather than being the exclusive possession of any one religion, and to see that all bigotry and fanaticism are anti-God.

I used to give private coaching to the children of an extremely wealthy Arab businessman in Kensington. One day he came into the room where I was teaching one of his boys. 'My son tells me that you are a Christian minister and that your church needs re-carpeting and there is no money. Buy what you need, and send me the bill.'

It was not the financial implications that astounded me; it was his spiritual generosity. Here was a devout follower of Islam contributing several thousand pounds to the refurbishment of a place of worship for followers of a different creed. There was no alienation here, no racial segregation or religious dismissiveness. There was only kindness.

Alienation can only end when Muslims give carpets to Christians and Christians pick up the bill for prayer mats. Pray that such a day becomes a reality before alienation and intolerance ravage God's world beyond repair.

Free us from prejudice, Lord, and let us overflow with your compassion. Amen.

21

Imagination

Matthew 1.18
The Birth of Jesus

Without imagination there would be no Christmas story. The religious myth, with its three kings, the startled shepherds, the mellifluous choir of angels and the birth in the stable, is the work of a visionary. Behind it in the dim, distant past lies a literary artist who has entranced thousands down the ages.

Imagination is the ingredient that turns the mundane world into a place of startling wonder and perpetual interest. Without it there would be no Panama Canal, no aeroplanes, radios or bicycles. It also fires the aesthetic world, and was the driving force behind the unsurpassable paintings of Raphael and, more recently, the church architecture of Gaudí and Le Corbusier.

With no imagination we would be a bookless world; such treasures as *Tess of the D'Urbervilles*, *Crime and Punishment*, *Sons and Lovers* and *War and Peace* would not exist. So too with music, which evolves from the constant input of human imagination and inventiveness. It is one of mankind's gifts.

Back in my student days, when money was scarce, I took a job as night-watchman with a security firm. My work dress was serge trousers, blouse jacket and peaked cap, complete with watchman's clock, truncheon and whistle. One December I was given the Christmas Eve shift in a furniture factory on Silver Street in north London. How could I possibly celebrate this most sublime of Christian festivals in a darkened, creepy factory at dead of night? The day guard departed, and I sat down to a mug of tea, bored, and nervous of the 'night demons'.

As the hours ticked by, the night became transfigured. I took my watchman's clock for the first round and heard the sound of slurred, blurred voices coming from an inn beyond the perimeter fence. Surely this must be the Christmas shepherds, searching for the inn that contained 'a saviour who is Christ the Lord'.

Out in the yard snow was settling between the darkened piles of timber. Then came a glimpse of burning coals, the blast of a whistle and an enfolding cloud of steam as the night sleeper from King's Cross to Edinburgh roared past, its lights aglow.

What was this unexpected vision, this brightness in the gloom of night? Surely it was no less than the choir of angels, hurrying on its way to distant Bethlehem from the heavenly regions.

In the typing pool, machines lay eerily shrouded, and the faint smell of perfume drifted in the air. On one desk was a photograph of a young mother and father cuddling a small child. God was smiling on me in that lonely typing pool. This was no less than the holy family cosseting their young child. In the wood-drying room a pile of planks had fallen in an odd, rectangular shape. I peered again, feeling the sharp scent of glue in my nose, the sweet smell of drying wood. I looked again. Yes, there was the manger; and that bundle of cloths thrown there casually by one of the workmen was the swaddled child.

In the reeking darkness of the machine shop was a Father Christmas, crudely made from offcuts of wood. A pile of make-believe parcels lay strewn at his feet. Another vision here: this time it was the three kings with their refractory camels and precious gifts, searching for they knew not what. Outside in an agate-cold sky a thousand stars twinkled, and I knew that one had guided them.

That night the Christmas story burgeoned and shaped itself out of the darkness. When morning broke and my relief arrived, I slipped into a neigh-bouring church to hear the early morning Mass and knew that there had been glory in that deserted factory.

If our sense of God becomes dim, our faith no more than a fragile hope, our vision stultified, we might well turn to Joseph Mary Plunkett's vision-ary poem 'I See His Blood upon the Rose', which imagines the divine presence everywhere. For him the red rose in the garden is Christ's blood, the stars God's all-glorious eyes. The snow and rain are His tears, the flowers reflect His face and the singing birds are His voice. Rocks are His words, and all pathways are trodden by Him. 'His strong heart stirs the ever-beating sea,/ His crown of thorns is twined with every thorn,/ His cross is every tree.'

Imagination is a blessed gift. Its luminous creativ-ity enables us to see the world in a transformed light. Use it, and you will see the divine sparking out from all that touches your path.

Enrich our vision, Lord, till it is irradiated
like light through a stained-glass window.
Amen.

22

Re-routing

Matthew 2.1–13
The kings return by another way

T. S. Eliot paints an imaginary picture of the coming of the three kings, in the cold – the dead of winter was not the most clement of seasons for travelling. The camels were sore-footed and galled, refusing at times to continue the absurd journey. The wise men hankered for their summer palaces and *houris* bringing sweetmeats. Hostility met them on the way: dirty villages offered them precarious safety, and money-grabbing local innkeepers tore at their purse-strings.

The Biblical picture is both more grandiose and more ethereal. It reads like a fairy tale. The kings are depicted as sages, coming from who-knows-where, travelling to a remote village. They follow a star, and, magically, it leads them to Palestine and a stable. Just to add sparkle, they bring gifts of priceless worth to present to the king of whom they have heard. The whole myth is a delight for head teachers wanting to end the Christmas term with a nativity play.

Here then is a picturesque legend, and it delights our senses to read it. But it is a throwaway line that holds the theological meat: 'And they departed to their own country by another way.' In other words, encountering the Holy God totally altered their religious convictions, moved the parameters of their philosophy and broadened their spiritual quest. The old road they had travelled was dug up and thrown away, and new vistas opened before them. This was a dramatic moment, a spiritual *bouleversement* that must have rocked them to the core. As Eliot puts it, they are 'no longer at ease here, in the old dispensation'.

Joseph Conrad's novella *Heart of Darkness* is another parable of re-routing. Charles Marlow is captain of a river steamboat working for an ivory-trading company. At a remote and barely accessible inland station lives a man called Kurtz. Legends abound concerning Kurtz's lack of sanity and corrupted vision of life. At times he takes on a skin of unreality, a devilish patina. For the indigenous population he has become a god.

Marlow's voyage slowly turns into a crusade to find the mysterious Kurtz. Innumerable hardships mark his journey through a plague-infested jungle. Often the terrain is shrouded in dense mist. For the reader there is a brooding sense that all is not well, that something sick and festering lies ahead. Indeed it does.

As they near Kurtz's camp, ominous events proliferate. Marlow's party come across a memo, written by Kurtz, referring to the natives. Its words are unsettling: 'Exterminate the brutes.' In the jungle, Marlow passes a gang of slaves, heads bowed, blistered, broken feet dragging in the sapping heat. Behind all these misgivings lies true corruption. Kurtz's protective palisade is studded with black heads spiked onto poles. Evil swirls in the forest.

During the final deathbed scene, Kurtz whispers four words that have been pondered over by countless scholars. 'The horror! The horror!'

In my mind, there is no doubt as to their meaning. Kurtz, knowing death to be imminent, is returning by another way. He is facing up to the reality of the evil he has inflicted upon the tropical forest.

Failure to constantly re-route our lives means that we have fossilized our creeds, our spirituality, our ethics and our prayer life. We believe ourselves to have arrived at the goal, our spiritual destination. There is a great sadness in this, for it means that we have abandoned the journey prematurely and taken on the self-satisfaction of thinking that we have come a long way. That teeters on the edge of both pride and piety.

Faith is the continuing search in life for glimpses of God, and it is a journey that never ends. To rephrase it, faith is not a voyage into certainty but the reverse. It is to launch out courageously into the unknown, letting life be our tutor and discovering unexpected jewels as the years slip past.

The Godward journey is exhilarating, exciting, ever-expanding, full of endless possibilities and embroidered with the light of fresh discoveries. To claim that we have discovered God is to live with a fallacy. What we have found will not be God but an idol of our own making.

One of the ancient spiritual masters, Dionysius the Areopagite, expressed it like this: 'Unto this darkness which is beyond light we pray.'

Happy voyaging into the unknown and, like the kings, may you return by another way. But venture out boldly, for God is at the helm.

God, the pathway to your kingdom is winding and narrow. Take our hands that we lose not the way. Amen.

23

Guilt

Matthew 27:5
Judas hangs himself

I have always felt sympathy for Judas and picture him searching for a length of rope and a low-slung tree branch. His exit from the world must have been an unholy synthesis of guilt, fear, shame, tears and despair.

One of the most frequent doorstep comments heard by the visiting parson is 'I'm afraid we don't go to church, Vicar.' This riposte marks the tip of an iceberg of submerged guilt, of all kinds, that bedevils society. Put guilt on the dissecting table, and its ugliness is revealed. It is shot through with self-loathing; and all hatred – whether directed at oneself or at another – is undesirable. Add to that the pinch of self-aggrandizement that often accompanies guilt and you get a malignant mix. 'Far from being insignificant, my sins are so important that they warrant the attention of God – even his wrath.' The scene is set for a spiritual ego-trip.

It is hard to screw any plus points out of guilt. Dwelling on it is a profligate use of time, a wallowing in our own nastiness. Better by far to help out at the senior citizens' annual fête. That is at least adding a pennyworth of help to the world.

More sinister is the malevolent power of guilt to fragment us internally. It sets up an uneasy tension between what we are and what we consider we should be. St Paul wrestled with just this dichotomy. His senses were permanently at war with his spiritual nature. If this were just a personal struggle, its damage would be limited. But it spills over into society for, if we hate ourselves, it is hard for us to love others, and our vision of the world outside and our behaviour towards it is warped and soured.

If guilt is so harmful and crippling, the obvious answer is to relegate it to the rubbish heap. That is easier said than done, for it sticks like epoxy glue. The church is not above reproach here, and in the past it has retained power by inducing guilt: yes, you have sinned grievously, but there is a way out, and we alone possess the magic elixir – confess to God, and the priest (as God's intermediary) will pronounce the words of divine absolution. It is a vicious circle of entrapment, and a subtle one at that.

There are various well-trodden roads for expunging guilt, such as the psychiatrist's couch, the doctor's tablets or a dialogue with the psychotherapist. But counselling does not suit everybody. For some, it is too much an invasion of personal space; and the doctor's arsenal has little to offer other than anti-depressant tablets. What about offloading guilt on to other people, as can happen in prison, where the murderer points a finger at the sex offender and says, 'At least I am not as bad as him'? This is no more than self deception.

We do not need to stay permanently in a pool of self-hatred. There is an escape hatch in remorse. Unlike guilt, remorse is upbeat and positive. It starts with contrition, burgeons into expiation and is finalized in resolve. To put it another way: feel sorry, put matters right as far as possible and move on. This shifts the suffocating intolerance and self-loathing of guilt away from ourselves and brings in a breath of fresh air from the outside world. Sometimes all that is needed is an apology, a settlement of outstanding debts, a request for forgiveness or a kiss. Having done all in our power to rectify the past, we can move into the future. Yes, that act was shabby – but I'll try to make a better showing next time round.

What about the deep-seated guilt that springs not from a peccadillo but from a heinous wrongdoing? You cannot write that off like a bad debt. Even in this twilight zone all is not lost. We have to start by facing an unpalatable truth: the past is irredeemable. What we have done is history, immutable and ineradicable. It may be that the only expiation we can offer the victim is an acceptance of the statutory punishment meted out by the law. Once our guilt has been transformed into genuine remorse and we have faced the music of justice, rebirth becomes a possibility.

This is precisely what happens in Dostoevsky's novel *Crime and Punishment*. Encouraged by the young prostitute Sonia, Raskolnikov – the penniless student who murdered the old sweetshop woman – finally yanks himself out of an endless circle of recrimination. He makes public confession of his crime in the town square, and Sonia promises to share his punishment in Siberia, the hell to which he has been banished.

At that point his guilt loses its demonic hold and he experiences 'a presentiment of future resurrection and a new life'.

I thank God, the all-loving, for the possibility – and sometimes the actuality – of our remorse.

*Blessed Lord, free us from the destructive
power of guilt, and show us the way
to remorse. Amen.*

24

Gender

John 4.9

*How is it that you, a Jew, ask a drink of me,
a woman of Samaria?*

Jesus had no time for political correctness. Here he
is speaking at the village well to a woman he did
not know. Just to rub the message in, he asks her for
a drink of water. To crown it all, she is a Samaritan,
and respectable Jews did not have dealings with
outcasts, or drink water polluted by female hands.

Jesus was on the side of the progressives, and
this was a slap in the face for the reactionaries. His
actions carry more than a hint of gender equality,
which is surprising considering that the encounter
took place two thousand years ago.

My boarding-school days were onerous and
crushing, and I did not fit the expected pattern.
Success on the rugby field, prowess on the athlet-
ics track and good teamwork were the marks of
a successful pupil, and I rebelled against it all. My

interests were wild flowers, butterflies and poetry, none of which suited the exclusively masculine outlook of the school. Beatings were frequent and were part of the process of toughening us up. Bullying and abuse were rife, but we took a deep breath and stuck it out; if we had reported it to a master, that would have signified weakness and effeminacy, and life for a junior boy who told tales and bucked the system would have been hell ten times over.

Emotion was frowned upon, tears a disgrace. The driving force of boarding school for boys in the 1940s was 'to make a man of you'. This is where the educational authorities had it all wrong. The psychologist C. G. Jung claimed that every female persona had a male part within, and in every male was a female persona struggling to get out. The intention should have been to nurture and enrich both the male and female parts, and to produce boys who were well balanced. In fact, the school turned out pupils who were emotionally stunted. It left a legacy of male superiority, and any suggestion of gender equality would have been laughed out of the window.

Only recently has the concept of male dominance broken down in the church, and even now there are pockets of resistance, sometimes fired by somewhat spurious theological arguments.

When gender is applied to our concept of God, the entire theological system goes awry. Sigmund Freud was right on target when he pointed out that we formulate a concept of God who is a stern father figure, keeping a strong rein on our *id*, that flirtatious, mischievous part of the subconscious that bubbles up every so often.

Having established this figure, we then clothe it with attributes and build a character who judges, forgives, views our misdeeds sternly, punishes and frowns at immorality. What we have ended up with is not God but an anthropomorphic image that we have sculpted.

For various reasons, the concept of an exclusively male God dies hard. It has been used as a symbol of power. Priests offering the Mass are the male representatives of Christ; an injection of femininity into this scenario upends tradition and involves power-sharing. Not everybody is prepared to do that. On top of that is the uneasy feeling that any hint of womanliness in the God concept smacks of heathen goddesses such as Astarte or Diana.

We need to start from square one and view God as beyond gender, far above our squabblings and petty disagreements. The mystery of the divine cannot be couched in human terms, nor can his personality be entrapped by our inadequate images or stereotypes.

God is neither male nor female but is unbounded love and holiness, far beyond our human reckoning. As Hildegard of Bingen said, 'It is easier to gaze into the sun than into the face of the mystery of God. Such is its beauty and its radiance.' To cut God down to size, to attempt to enclose his divinity in arcane terminology, is to miss his glory. Arrogantly to secularize his holiness is to attempt the impossible.

The German mystic Rilke illustrates the restrictive, misleading nature of God-images. Time and again we take the same gold colour from the paint box to add to our distorted vision of God:

Piously we produce our images of you
till they stand around you like a thousand walls.
And when our hearts would simply open,
our fervent hands hide you.

So bow down silently this Lent before the unknown, unknowable God. Let yourself be suffused with divine light and peace; and with God be the rest.

Lord, break down the walls that hide us from your presence, and open our eyes to your dazzling glory. Amen.

25

Abortion

Mark 2.16–18
Herod massacres the innocents

The prosaic words with which the gospel writer describes the slaughter of all the two-year-old boy children belies its innate horror, but it gives King Herod an infamous place alongside the world's most callous dictators. Picasso's mural of *Guernica* floats into my mind. It was painted in response to the bombing of the innocent civilians of the town, and it is one of the most moving and powerful war paintings the world has seen. It uses a palette of grey, black and white in order to recreate a scene from which every fleck of colour has been drained. Depicted are a horse with a gaping wound, and a dismembered soldier. A figure trapped by fire on all sides adds to the desolation. What stands out is a woman grieving over a dead child that she is holding in her arms.

The lives of children are of supreme importance, so I thought carefully when the woman sitting huddled in my study said, 'Do you think I should have an abortion, Vicar?' She was distressed and embarrassed and heavy with grief. Three days earlier her partner had shot himself because of massive debts, leaving her pregnant.

Together we went through all the arguments for seeking a termination. The child would be fatherless. There was no immediate family waiting in the wings to give support. She had a career to follow, and a mountain of unpaid bills. Motherhood would mean bankruptcy, homelessness and penury. On top of that it seemed unfair to bring into the world a child whose father had taken his own life. It was not a good legacy.

There were counter-indications. Some surgeons are understandably reluctant to perform abortions on healthy foetuses. At that time, it would probably have meant an expensive private clinic, which she could ill afford; nor did she relish the clinical approach to life offered by such establishments.

Guilt was another factor to fit into the dialectic. As a hospital chaplain I had seen long-standing regret and depression following abortions.

She threw the ball back into my court. 'What do you advise, Reverend?' It was an unacceptable question, a passing of the moral buck. She wanted to offload the gruelling burden of choice on to me. That way she could not lose. If I rejected abortion outright as immoral and godless, she could blame me rather than herself for any future detrimental outcome if she should decide to keep the child. If I backed the abortion proposal, her conscience was off the hook – she could claim that she had done it with the church's approval.

Where religion is concerned, it is vital to maintain freedom of choice. A faith that is based on a set of prohibitions or a code of moral injunctions should be approached warily. The shouldering of ethical decisions cannot be farmed out. So also a spirituality that requires its members to subscribe to a set of creedal assertions is snatching back the right of the individual to choose what to believe, and how to behave. We are back to the Victorian father addressing his son here. 'Why should I do it, Father?' 'Because I say so.'

One of the blessings of our humanity is that we have a conscience. To opt out of using such a priceless gift is irresponsible. Of course there are immense dangers here. We may make ill-guided decisions. Our thinking may be warped or illogical. On occasion we may follow a course of action so unsociable and unwise that we end up before the magistrate. But if we allow the church or the nanny state, the media or popular opinion, to become our conscience we lose our moral integrity. So I could not answer the question 'Should I have an abortion, Vicar?' Only she could do that, after reflecting on the pros and cons of the situation that we had thrashed out earlier.

Without free will, we would be hapless creatures staggering across the world, predestined to follow a prescribed course of action, helpless to influence events. Free will is a great gift. But it comes with strings attached, and one of those is the agony of choosing. We cannot evade it or ignore its demands. For the young woman in my study there was no easy way out. She had to make her choice, and take on board the consequences.

Our freedom to choose is both our human glory and our cross. But Christ never did maintain that his way was a bed of roses.

Life is your greatest gift, Lord: let us never sour or diminish it. Amen.

26

Silence

Mark 3.7
Jesus withdraws to the sea

There are no glittering candles here; no whiff of incense in the still air. Weather-beaten stone stairways lead upwards to nowhere. Gaping doorways, once heavy and studded, offer views of massed clouds. These are the ruins of the great Cistercian Abbey of Jervaulx, and I have come here to find silence. I am in good company, because Jesus often fled the world.

At first it hovers uneasily, for we are used to doing rather than being. There is an irritating urge to fidget. Eyes wander; ears become acutely aware of disruptive sounds. Thoughts whirl like a sandstorm. A tractor throbs and turns hay, and the shuffle of feet on a nearby gravel path intrude. But soon the silence steadies, settles and becomes palpable, threaded with strands of the holy. Gradually it engulfs all distraction, subsuming it until even the raucous croaking from the rookery melds into the quietness.

Journey further into the silence with T. S. Eliot – 'We must be still and still moving/Into another intensity,/ For a further union, a deeper communion' – and curious things begin to happen. Time changes its nature. It is no longer linear, extending from the moment I parked my car until I take my place among the ruins. It has become motionless: a single point with no past, no future, that holds me tight in its embrace.

Sight is enriched, and the patch of cow parsley clinging to the base of a stone buttress takes on a colour and a lace-like beauty that had previously eluded me. Perception is clarified, and I am no longer an outsider observing this tumbled ruin but I am a part of it, at one with its ancient history, sad at its downfall. Hearing has become more acute, so that the sound of insects, the rustle of leaves, all point to a harmony and a complexity in nature that awakens the seeds of wonder.

There is no ongoing dialogue with a personal God here, no creedal assertions to make, no dogmatic announcements to drag the mind into an inward, intellectual discourse. The silence has cosseted me through and beyond all that. In the inimitable words of the Welsh poet R. S. Thomas, 'the silence/ Holds with its gloved hand/The wild hawk of the mind.'

At this point of heightened awareness, a hidden dynamic begins its transforming work, reshaping, reorienting what Paul Tillich called 'the depths of our being'. The silence is a focus point from which a new vision emerges. We see our perplexing, apparently meaningless and often brutal world not with dismay but with a renewed hope. A great weight has been lifted, and calm folds us comfortingly. Silence has become the womb from which we can toss out onto the world holistic words such as 'peace', 'gratitude', 'compassion', 'joy' and 'love'.

We have lost the art of being silent, and with it much of the intensity of silent contemplation. Greek beaches in their one-time rugged splendour and isolation are nowadays torn apart by loudspeakers relaying pop music. Building sites are alive with full-blast radios, and our houses are disturbed by electrical devices and background noise.

There is purpose in all this, and intent. Unaccustomed silence brings fear in its wake. It forces us to confront what is unpalatable in our lives, and so we run from it: 'My marriage is slowly disintegrating'; 'I am trapped in a job that carries no fulfilment'; 'Life holds no meaning for me.'

This can easily turn into self-deprecation, with its implications that we are inadequate or unlovable. So unbearable are these unwelcome reflections that we blot them out with noise and busyness.

There is a hidden paradox here, for the silence that opens the gate to unease is also the pathway leading to inner peace and tranquillity. If we can find the courage to carry our fears and desperation into the silence, we will find that our sour vision of the world and ourselves has become altogether kinder and more optimistic, because we are tapping into the eternity that is God.

I left the ruins of the once majestic abbey with the words of the German mystic and poet Rainer Maria Rilke ringing in my ears:

I come home from the soaring
in which I lost myself.
I was song, and the refrain which is God
is still roaring in my ears . . .
I'd gone very far, as far as the angels,
and high, where light thins into nothing.

Silence had brought me to the edge of that luminous barrier lying between heaven and earth. Do not underestimate its power.

Lord Christ, hold us in the depths of your silence, and let your enfolding love keep us safe. Amen.

27

Eternity

John 11.25
He who believes in me,
though he die yet shall he live

'Do you believe in life after death, Vicar?' People look aghast if you propound a theory of agnosticism – not knowing. You can imagine the comeback: 'Don't you believe in the creed? But you say it every week.' I would maintain that creeds are not obligatory beliefs inscribed in stone with the stamp of divine approval but a set of christological, theistic hypotheses from which we try to draw out our own truth.

The concept of eternity has its drawbacks. When we speak of something 'taking an eternity', we are implying that the situation is flecked with frustration, boredom and annoyance. You can imagine the traveller standing in a queue at Gatwick complaining that boarding is taking an eternity.

It also has downbeat, nineteenth-century overtones and a disparaging ring. The Victorian gentry used it as a carrot to help labourers through a life that was dreary and unrewarding, hence the morbid hymn:

A few more years shall roll,
A few more seasons come,
And we shall be with those that rest,
Asleep within the tomb.

It paints life as a desperate endurance course. We must grit our teeth and survive it as best we can, as if it were a particularly severe military boot camp for defaulters.

So, does eternal life exist or is it a fable holding out the promise of a non-existent nirvana beyond the pain of this life? There is one way in which we are all eternal, and it is written into the burial service. When the body is committed to the ground, the priest says, 'earth to earth, ashes to ashes, dust to dust'. The coffin is either lowered into the earth or surrendered to the cleansing fire of the crematorium. In this sense our ashes, our dust, return to the earth and become part of the ground from which new life can spring. They become the forerunner of a future creation. It is a comforting thought that we return to the womb of mother earth, from which we once emerged.

In Leo Tolstoy's great work *War and Peace*, Prince Andrei muses as he lies dying on his sick-bed: 'Without haste or agitation he awaited what was coming.' Interfused with this waiting is a strange lightness. A flower of eternal, unfettered love instantly unfolds itself in his soul, and he no longer fears death. Then, through a haze of fever, he looks up and finds that his dearest love, Natasha, has come into the sick-room and is knitting beside him. She provides a soft tranquillity, and he wants to weep for joy. As death draws nearer, he says, 'Everything is united by love alone. Love is God and to die means that I, a particle of love, shall return to the general and eternal source.' His is a peaceful death untrammelled by pain and regret, acted out in the presence of his lover. Maybe that is eternal life – a few blessed moments at the end, when an inner peace is found.

In his poem 'Prospice', Robert Browning speaks of another death, a passing that he wants to meet with courage and fortitude. He has always been a fighter, and this last fight is to be the best. He wants to taste it in its wholeness, even if there are within it elements of pain, darkness and cold. The poem ends in ravishing verse. There comes that moment when the black minute ends and the raging of the elements and the raving fiend voices die away into a hush. At that moment his journey changes. The new life 'shall become first a peace out of pain./Then a light, then thy breast,/ O thou soul of my soul! I shall clasp thee again,/ And with God be the rest!' The gates of life have closed, and he sees the Christ stand.

I do not know my ending, nor can I guess its essence or nature. Perhaps it will be my dust returning to the earth in a kind of cosmic eternity. Or it may be an unimaginable state that lies beyond all human conceiving.

The mystery will not be unfolded until my dying moment. That said, the words of the seventeenth-century poet and mystic Angelus Silesius take all fear of death from me. God is 'the deepest well from which all rises, grows,/ Boundless ocean back into which all flows'.

I pray that the boundless ocean will receive me with love and mercy when my time comes.

O God, king of the swelling oceans, when our time comes, draw us into the tide of your eternal life. Amen.

28

Agnosticism

Acts 17.22–3
The Athenians pray to an unknown God

Part of the appeal of faith is that it gives a *raison d'être* in our disturbingly uncertain world, a security that holds us firm. Follow the Christian path in staunch faith and we will receive blessing in this life and happiness thereafter.

But it comes with a caution. Any faith journey leads to a bottleneck: a religious system with its own rules, assertions and strictures. That presages mental stagnation. Why question Christ's resurrection if it has all been done for us in the creed and gospels? Why work out for ourselves a system of morals when it is written large in the Ten Commandments?

There is another risk. Faith can lead to divisiveness. We all have our own theological beliefs, and in the western world Christianity still tops the list. Worse still, faith can shape-shift into a far more sinister beast: bigotry. The destructive fanaticism that comes from unbending certainty has the power to rend the world apart.

So have we got the destination all wrong? Should the spiritual journey be heading not for unwavering belief but for agnosticism? Is the goal not certainty but unknowing? There are many points in its favour. The man of faith has reached a terminus. He has arrived by following the traditional route of creed, scripture, doctrine and prayer, and the journey is over. Not so for the agnostic. His travels are continuous, ever-changing, unpredictable and unfettered by orthodoxy. Who knows what spiritual discoveries may lie ahead?

There is another gain. Once you embrace 'not knowing', narrow-mindedness fades into oblivion. Humankind is perceived not as a posse of religious rivals out to get us but as a band of respected fellow explorers.

Agnosticism brings with it a tremendous spiritual kick. Because we see the universe as an ultimate mystery, our sense of the numinous is sharpened. Holiness dances everywhere. Our respect for the cosmos becomes profound. We will want to hug devotees of other faiths, not spit fire and brimstone at them.

There are drawbacks, but they will not deter the firm-hearted. It is easy to get cold feet when launching out into the soaring, unknown regions of agnosticism. All the old props have gone, and this is a solo journey. Again we often end up in a cul-de-sac. We try one philosophy, and it leads nowhere. So we start all over again, always searching, ever seeking new fields and a more enlightened concep-tion of the Holy One.

In his novel *The Abbé Mouret's Transgression*, Émile Zola paints a picture of Serge Mouret, a young, dedicated but cold priest. He recalls his pure, virginal days in the seminary. He enjoys a life of perfect obedience. As for prayer, an hour before the statue of the Virgin Mary is as nothing. But he falls ill, and Dr Pascal sends him to recuperate at the run-down estate of Pardou, which has a garden full of lush plants run rife. It is an exemplar of the garden of Eden, full of primal beauty, cajoling and unsettling the priest. In the stifling heat he falls in love with Albine, a young girl who runs wild among the flowers. There beneath a canopy of trees they kiss and make love. It is transformative for the priest. He feels more masculine, his senses become more acute.

Later he confesses to Jesus his love for Albine, but God remains silent. Torn apart by his conflict-ing emotions he stands up in church and makes a soul-searing declaration. 'There is nothing, nothing,

God does not exist.' He meets once more with his beloved and she talks of their future life together, but he speaks only of his love for the church. After a tortured spell of intellectual tussling, he has reverted to the severe, unbending priest. When night comes, Albine, deserted, gathers great handfuls of flowers and locks herself in the bedroom. She dies of asphyxiation, overcome by their stifling scent. The garden of Eden has lost its pristine glory.

Ironically the sinning, agnostic priest, Abbé Mouret, is nearer to God, more filled with love, richer in prayer, than the hard, unrelenting believer he has become.

To be agnostic is to be in good company. The fourteenth-century mystic–parson who wrote *The Cloud of Unknowing* was blunt. 'Do what you will, this cloud remains between you and your God and stops you from seeing him in the clear light of rational understanding.' I reckon his signpost was pointing in the right direction.

Hidden God, on our journey may we find
you in the darkness and in the light. Amen.

29

Transfiguration

Mark 9.23
Jesus is transfigured

Rembrandt had the gift of transfiguring faces. He took the old, wrinkled visage of a woman, lace-collared, and with consummate skill illuminated it so that it became a work of beauty. Transfiguration is the process whereby we come to view people and things in a deeper dimension. On the mountain, the face of Christ was radically altered, his features shone white and his clothing glistened. This was not a conjuring trick, a sleight of hand that turned him chalk-coloured. In metaphorical language it describes how, for the first time, the disciples saw beneath the superficial humanity of Jesus to something deeper. What changed was not reality but their perception of it.

Some years ago I had a parish that comprised several of the old Cleveland ironstone villages. Every autumn the potato-pickers arrived with a ramshackle procession of caravans, wheezing trucks, giant Calor gas cylinders, chained dogs and children running wild. It was the prelude to six weeks of back-breaking work gathering mud-encased potatoes from frozen ground and dropping them into sacks. Local opinion was somewhat scathing. Assumptions were made without any evidence: they were thieves, leavers of rubbish, not to be trusted in any way, doorstep fiddlers. There was an element of fear too, and nobody wanted to cross them. No doubt they would be handy with knives, and those dogs would scare off a platoon of soldiers.

But they were a part of my parish, and the instructions in the Book of Leviticus pull no punches. 'The stranger who sojourns with you shall be to you as the native among you and you shall love him as yourself.' So one cold September afternoon I donned a pair of wellies and a thick anorak, grabbed a thumbstick against an attack by the dogs and opened the field gate. Urchins stared; faces peered from behind curtains. Then a van door opened and a woman emerged, backed by two beautiful teenage girls.

'I want to ask you something, Father. Do you do christenings?' The faint Irish brogue faltered. 'Only we are Catholics and I feel badly with the girls not being done.' They were constantly on the move, had no parish, and clergy were unwilling to baptize children they would never see again. I told her that I was a Church of England priest, and her answer was a lesson in reunion. 'It's all the same, isn't it.' So I talked to those unlettered, brazen girls, telling them about Christ's teaching, and the day came when they tottered across to the font, wearing shoes for the first time ever, their feet a sea of pain. Giggling, bashful, pink-cheeked and proud, they bent over the water and dedicated their lives to the Almighty.

After the ceremony I returned with them to the caravan and their father sang me Romany songs as he lay, well oiled, on the caravan sofa. Mother and girls served me biscuits with tea in exquisite, fine china cups.

Travelling folk are aliens, constantly entering a strange land, often unwelcome and distrusted. They have no permanent home, no mother church. But I had seen them transfigured. They had become persons, graceful, grateful, and imbued with a need for the spiritual.

Transfiguration requires us to look at the lad working in the garage, his hands oil-smeared, blue overalls soaked in grease. He might be fresh from a remand home; he certainly has a mother and father, and perhaps a girlfriend. That girl working in the supermarket has a name. You can see it on her badge. Speak a few words of kindness and view her not as an employee but as a work of God's glorious creation with all the potential to love and be loved. Look at her in a transfigured light and give a few seconds of time to utter a silent prayer to the creator that he will hold her tight in his never-failing embrace.

Mechthild of Magdeburg was a thirteenth-century mystic who had a transfiguring experience when she was a child and perceived 'all things in God and God in all things'. Her work *The Flowing Light of the Godhead* describes the union between God and his beloved children. Her words ring loud and clarion clear as she sees all humanity as immersed in God, transfigured in roseate light. 'See and taste the Flowing Godhead through thy being. Feel the Holy Spirit moving and compelling thee within the flowing fire and light of God.'

That day when we can see the whole world and those within it bathed in the incandescent fire of God's love will mark the coming of the kingdom.

Lord, may we search untiringly for the incandescent light of your glory, even in the dark places that we fear. Amen.

30

Peace

Ephesians 2.17
He came and preached peace

Peace is the salve the world needs. Human trafficking, dictatorships and the great surge of materialism overtaking the world have driven it away. The poet Gerard Manley Hopkins sees it differently. For him peace is like a wild wood-dove, always roaming around, elusive and impossible to entrap. He utters a desolate cry, 'Why don't you come to me?' Although he admits that peace does come sometimes, it is only piecemeal, unsatisfactory, and ringed by alarms of war and the daunting tide of human enormity. The stark conclusion reached by the poet is that we cannot find peace in the world unless we first find it in ourselves and then pour it out onto humanity. Only then will life 'plume' into peace.

Today's world is alive with mistrust, threats, nuclear dice-throwing and war. It all makes Plato's concept of absolute good seem pie-in-the-sky. As for

Immanuel Kant's belief that humanity in its entirety has embedded in it 'a moral law within', the whole idea seems empty and doubtful.

There is one road that has unfailingly led me towards the ephemeral, ever-distant goal of peace, and it is found in the work of the Jewish philosopher Martin Buber. His work *I and Thou*, published in 1923 and hailed in its day as 'a great event in the religious life of the west', has lost none of its persuasiveness and power, and it offers a cohesive world-view on which to build a framework of peace.

For him all existence is encounter, and the fundamental way we engage with the world and encounter it is through the primary relational term 'I–It'. What this means is that we view people and things as objects to be acquired, categorized, possessed and exploited. In my mind is the tragedy of a lorryload of illegal immigrants who suffocated to death in the dark confines of an airless, locked truck. They were regarded as a source for making money, a commodity to be traded in. That is the I–It relationship at its most devastating and terrible. In essence it is no more than a selfish monologue: 'How can the world satisfy my lust for power and possessions? What can I claw back from life to feather my nest?' It is a nihilistic philosophy that brings in its wake grief, contempt and gross greed. There can be no place for I–It in a Christian society.

All is not lost, however, for there is a second primary relational word: 'I–Thou': an encounter at the deepest level with humanity, nature, art and existence. This turns our perception of the world upside down. No longer do we treat it as something that is there for our convenience; rather, we view it with respect and wonder. Take this on board and we no longer see a tree purely as a source of timber, something to be hacked down in the rainforest for financial gain. We become bound up with it. Think of the anguish with which Gerard Manley Hopkins views the felling of poplar trees on the bank of the River Thames. 'O if we but knew what we do/When we delve or hew – /Hack and rack the growing green!' For him, the trees had become a 'Thou'.

In *Cider with Rosie*, Laurie Lee describes his first bite of the apple when he makes tentative love to Rosie as they drink cider under the haywain. 'Never to be forgotten, that first long secret drink of golden fire.' Then he speaks of Rosie's burning cheeks, which are never to be tasted again. For him, Rosie the village girl has been transfigured by the ecstasy of sexual attraction and budding love. She has emerged like a butterfly from a chrysalis and has become a 'Thou'.

I remember one summer's day in the burning heat of rural Greece. We had driven our car unwisely along a rock-strewn lane surrounded by crumbling walls and curious goats. Cicadas whirred in the olive trees. We were hopelessly lost. Then a dilapidated house came into view, and a woman came running out with a bunch of grapes. She was exercising that most beautiful of graces, Greek *philoxenia* – friendliness to strangers. Her face lit up, and she told us the way. No longer a stranger, she was a goatherd who radiated kindness and peace unreservedly.

If we translate all our encounters into an 'I–Thou' relationship, compassion, love and understanding will emerge, and peace will lie quietly in our hearts. Martin Buber's eloquent, spiritual–philosophical world-view has the potential to transform humanity. Try it, in the name of Christ.

May the radiant peace of Christ fill our hearts with joy. Amen.

31

Prayer

1 Thessalonians 5.16
Pray without ceasing

Prayer is a loaded word, open to misunderstanding. Trickiest of all is the prayer of intercession. It needs unpacking. In Ernest Hemingway's novel *A Farewell to Arms*, a young soldier is lying in the trenches at Fossalta, under bombardment. He is terrified, and in his desperation a prayer forms on his lips. 'Dear Jesus, if you will only keep me from getting killed, I'll do anything you say. I believe in you and I'll tell everybody in the world that you are the only thing that matters. Please, please, dear Jesus.'

But the next day he goes upstairs with a girl from the brothel, Villa Rosa, and he does not tell her about Jesus. Nor does he tell anybody else.

Nobody can blame the soldier for his cry to God at the moment of fear. What is wrong is his picture of the Lord. He assumes that God is a remote figure, dallying with human life, playing games with his creation. He is a god who is open to bargaining, and will save you if your prayer is sufficiently fervent. The soldier has anthropomorphized God, and turned him into an image of a superman.

At first sight, rejecting this perception might seem to knock intercessory prayer on the head. What it really does, however, is to rejig it. Instead of being reduced to a pleading, a twisting of God's arm, intercession evolves into something more meaningful and less self-centred. Intercessory prayer is a matter of holding, for example, a sick patient in the presence of God, tuning in to the aura of divine love that swirls around all hospital beds. We are asking for nothing, expecting nothing. Rather, we are trusting in the inexorable onward flow of life that is God's creativity at work.

Then there is the prayer of silence: wordless, shutting out the encroaching sound and fury of the world, resting peacefully in the glow of divine light. This is an art that the mystics learned long ago. Perhaps it is the most meaningful of all prayers, for it contains no weak, uncertain human input. We are handing ourselves over, body and soul, to the Almighty, and in return we are given an outpouring of grace and love.

Charles Wesley's theologically rich hymn 'O thou who camest from above' makes just this point. There is a reciprocal flame of love burning between God and the one who is praying. Wesley makes a plea, 'There let it for thy glory burn, with inextinguishable blaze, and trembling to its source return in humble prayer and fervent praise.' Pseudo-Dionysius, an early theologian, paints this beautifully: 'Unto this darkness which is beyond Light we pray that we may come.' For him, prayer is the process of approaching God, who lies beyond all perception and understanding.

St Paul takes the concept of prayer further in his extraordinary claim that we should pray without ceasing. Our immediate responses are negative: this is impossible; I am not that saintly; life does not allow time for that. But wait. Prayer can be seen as an existential colloquy, an ongoing dialogue with the world.

We slog our way to the summit of Helvellyn and exclaim, 'The view is wonderful.' That is the prayer of adoration.

As we lie in a hospital bed, longing to get better, fearing the treatment, we are making an unspoken plea to the Lord of the universe to treat us with a modicum of kindness. That too is prayer.

To be uplifted by music, transported by sexual union or moved by a child's school play is the prayer of appreciation and love. If we shop in a supermarket and send out sympathetic thoughts to the young woman in a wheelchair, we are praying.

All our dialogue has been transformed into prayer, and the entire day becomes a heartfelt inter-communication with the Holy God.

Does it work? I tried it out on a classroom of recalcitrant fifth-formers, telling them the haunting, devastating tale of miners trapped underground without water, light, warmth or hope. 'What did you feel?' I asked. Up shot the hands. 'Wicked. Awful to be shut up like that.' 'Made me cry.' On and on went the compassionate responses. At last I stared at the class and said, 'Then you were all praying.'

Turn every prosaic event of the day into a divine interchange. Then you will be praying without ceasing. Try it.

Come to us, Lord, in those moments of silent prayer so that we bubble up like a spring of fresh water. Amen.

32

Voyaging

2 Corinthians 11.25
Three times I suffered shipwreck

Our school chapel contained an eye-catching mural by Frank Brangwyn of St Paul being shipwrecked. Out of the brilliant, almost garish colouring a bold drawing emerges: a picture of the bearded figure stepping ashore, his feet touching the longed-for shingle. Paul was a great journeyer, and that is not surprising, because the Christian life is just that.

Chaucer's *Canterbury Tales* tell the individual stories of a group of disparate travellers setting out on a pilgrimage to Canterbury. A wide spectrum of raw life is contained in the tales. The bawdy yarns of the friar, the miller and the wife of Bath mingle with those of the physician and the parson. The squire and the knight introduce an element of chivalry. For all the members of this motley crew of travellers, however, with their drinking, ribaldry, flirtation and solemnity, life was a pilgrimage on which they were embarking, which they hoped would lead, sometimes indirectly, towards God. Whatever our background, calling, religious stance or political leanings, we are all setting off towards an unknown goal.

The American poet Walt Whitman had a tough life. He was the son of an alcoholic Quaker carpenter. One brother was sent to a mental home, and his sister suffered a disastrous marriage, while his younger brother turned to drink and married a woman of the streets. For Walt, life was a spiritual odyssey incorporating not only the early sources of Christianity in the Bible but also the core of all ancient religions. This ceaseless voyaging tosses him into a world of pristine beauty in which God's hand is descried: 'O vast Rondure, swimming in space,/ Cover'd all over with visible power and beauty'.

From this vision, two urgent questions emerge like a haunting refrain: 'Whither O mocking life?' and 'Wherefore unsatisfied soul?' The poet is asking what is the goal of this unpredictable, strange existence we have been given. Where is it heading, and what lies at the terminus?

For Whitman, the way forward lies in a marriage of the natural world and humankind, so that world history merges into a spiritual oneness connecting all races, past and present. So enticing is this dream that he is straining at the leash to embark: 'We can wait no longer, / We too take ship O soul.'

There is a paradox at the heart of this journey. Certainly at one level it brings happiness, peace, laughter and joy, but there are doubts and fears too as he confronts the mystery of the future. He shrivels nervously at the thought of God, and at the wonders of nature. And time, space and earth – those great imponderables – fill him with foreboding. But we must break free from the chains of the past and surge forward.

The springboard for Whitman's journey was the opening of the Suez Canal on 17 November 1869, and the new, faster route to India that it offered. In his poem 'Passage to India' he admits that the search for God requires intrepidity and a profound trust in the world, as well as courage to face what comes freshly into being each day: 'Sail forth – steer for the deep waters only, / Reckless, O soul, exploring, I with thee, and thou with me.'

His voyage takes him to a place unknown to any mariner, where none has ventured to go. It involves risking the ship, ourselves and all. But that is a small price to pay, and he ends with words of immense encouragement: 'O my brave soul! O farther, farther sail!'

This troubled poet has much to say about today's spiritual voyage. We cannot survive on our materialistic achievements alone, however notable they are. We must spiritualize our being and our creativity as well. Nor can we build a worthwhile world if it is spiked with intolerance and hate. We need to reawaken our sense of the wholeness of humanity. The world is a vast *rondure*, a cosmic entity, a glorious example of divine handiwork.

As to the nature of the voyage itself, he leaves us in no doubt. It is not a safe regression to the doctrinal beliefs of our individual faiths but a journey that takes on board novelty, and differing theological ideas. It hurls us out into a passage of discovery, heady with risk but finally safe, because we are sailing on God's seas.

Rethink the spiritual journey. Question every aspect of faith, search always for new paths and fresh visions of God's glory. Yes, it is a fearful and daunting journey, but would we expect the pathway towards the Lord of Light to be otherwise? Take heart too, for all the seas, rough, smooth, swelling or calm, are the work of the divine hand. What is more, that hand is on the ship's wheel.

When the journey is perilous, when doubts and weakness overcome us, do not forget us, Lord Christ. Amen.

33

Cosmology

Colossians 1.15–20
He is the image of the
invisible God

I recall endless theological college discussions, which went on for half the night. Often they revolved around the words 'Jesus is the divine Son of God', which we viewed from every conceivable angle. Did it make sense philosophically? Could it be proved empirically? Was it just playing with semantics? Most compelling, did it meet the requirement of reason, or did it imply that we had to put our intelligence on hold?

Those with an evangelical bent maintained that we had to swallow it hook, line and sinker. That was what the Bible said, and to question it would be to remove the foundations of the faith. Those with Anglo-Catholic leanings would refer back to the sacrament, and the presence of Christ in the sacrifice of the Mass. As for liberals, they were left with an uneasy feeling that this hurdle had to be met head-on and not sidestepped.

There are problems inherent in this statement. Scientifically and genetically it is an impossibility. Two separate personalities cannot be fused into one, other than in the case of mental illness. Semantically it is not possible to get beyond Wittgenstein's famous remark that 'the meaning of a word is its use'. On a less elevated level, it is hard to see how a Nazarene carpenter living two thousand years ago in a remote part of the Roman empire could aspire to be God. True, he was a brilliant ethicist and story-teller, and his compassion and powers of healing are not in dispute.

To say that the claim 'Jesus is the Son of God' is a paradox describes the nature of the statement, but it does not explain it. Years of house-to-house visiting and private chats with fellow clergy have made me realize that I am not alone in expressing this difficulty. It is more widespread than one might like to admit.

It may sound heretical, but my guess is that St Paul – that diehard Christian – also experienced searching moments of doubt. He rants on interminably about the law, sin and salvation, and frequently bursts into passages of sublime beauty and theological perceptivity, But, behind it all, what did he really think and believe?

To answer that, I have always turned to his epistle to the Colossians. There he puts forward a template diametrically opposed to the earthly man of Nazareth. Jesus has become 'the image of the invisible, God, the firstborn of all creation'. Not only that: 'All things were created though him and for him. He is before all things and in him all things hold together.' That is a weighty conclusion, which paints a radically new picture of Christ.

He has been 'cosmologized': Jesus has been transposed from his birthplace in Nazareth and given a universal, divine dimension. Paul seems to be saying that we need to look through and beyond the Nazarene woodworker, who is a symbol, an earth-bound image of the God who exists beyond all our human dimensions and thoughts. I can imagine Paul pointing to an image of Jesus and saying, 'This is not the end of the story. Christ is a pastiche of all that God is, namely unfathomable, unknowable, the Lord of Glory.' Far from belittling the Jesus of the gospels, this is an elevation of him to divine status, deftly accomplished by Paul so that it does not strain our reason.

How does this leave the miracles and parables of Jesus? The answer is: stronger than ever. If we view the marriage in Cana and the turning of water into wine as literal truth, we enter the field of fantasy. If, rather, we search it for meaning, it becomes an allegory of the richness that comes from an encounter with God.

Take the narrative of the loaves and fishes. It is incredible that a paltry helping of picnic food could feed a multitude. But the overwhelming fecundity of God's creation, which it underlines, is very real.

What of Jesus touching the dead son of the widow of Nain, and restoring him to life? Some can suspend rationality and believe it to be utter truth. Others will shake their heads as scripture battles with reason. For me, it is a picture story that I search for meaning. While it may or may not be historically true, it certainly contains truth, and it is part of my religious journey to try and discover just what that is. Is it a parable of compassion, an illustration of God's creative urge, or a pointer from Jesus of Nazareth to Christ, who is the image of the invisible God?

Part of life's excitement is the search for the divine. I never tire of it, and time and again I thrill at finding glimpses of his glory. So be like the man who took a spade, dug in the field and unearthed treasure. Happy hunting as you search the world for reflections of God's glory.

Startle us out of our apathy, Lord, and give us a fresh vision of your boundless love. Amen.

34

Ethics

Matthew 19.16
What good deed must I do to inherit eternal life?

'Is it right to steal bread from the baker to feed a starving child?' That old chestnut throws us straight into the muddy waters of ethics. I have tried most of the classical theories of ethics and found them wanting. Hedonism – the belief that pleasure is the greatest good – is crudely self-centred and rules out any spiritual element. Utilitarianism, or the greatest good for the greatest number, is a dream, and unworkable. For Kant, motivation was the key word: are our actions in tune with the universal moral law within? An inherent weakness clothes this theory. The moral law was in no way evident in Stalin's Russia or Pinochet's Chile. Does the Bible help?

The Ten Commandments were a set of rules drawn up to cope with the specific needs of the Hebrews wandering in the desert. They do not easily cross the barrier of culture. How do we honour our parents if they have lived dishonourably?

Jesus' words reflect the morality of his time and do not cover many of the ethical questions of our own day concerning drink, drugs, people-trafficking, same-sex marriages and genetic modification. In the end we are forced back into making our own decisions. There is no escape from that.

In 1955 Ruth Ellis was sentenced to death for killing her lover, a 25-year-old racing driver. She was a nightclub hostess. The Home Secretary refused to commute the sentence, and on the day of execution the prison governor had to call for police reinforcements around the main gates of Holloway Prison. Petitions were signed, prayers offered; and the House of Commons was informed that she had suffered a miscarriage ten days earlier, when her partner, David Blakely, punched her in the stomach.

On the day of the execution my school classroom was extraordinarily quiet. As nine o'clock struck there was total silence and a sense of shock. The rope noose had tightened, and Ruth Ellis was swinging by the neck. My ethical stance on hanging was sealed from that moment: it was not the act of a civilized society. That night in the dormitory after lights out, several boys wept. I was one of them.

Graham Greene's novel *The Power and the Glory* describes how an unnamed 'whisky priest' is wanted by the police. Roman Catholicism has been banned in Mexico, and the penalty for practising the faith is death. The priest is a broken man, sozzled from drink, the father of a child conceived with one of his parishioners, worn out by self-hatred and a sense of failure.

He meets up with an itinerant peasant who turns out to be Judas the betrayer.

The police try to flush him out by executing any villagers who provide him with food or help. After several episodes of near-capture, the priest escapes into neutral territory. The peasant tracks him down and tells him that there is a dying American murderer in the forest who wants a priest to hear his confession. The priest knows that it is a trap, but he makes one last heroic effort to honour his calling and, like Jesus, sets his face and heads for his Calvary.

His fear is full of pathos but it has a grandness about it. The lieutenant is closing the cell door when a scared voice breaks in. 'Lieutenant, you've seen people shot. Does the pain go on a long time?' 'No. No. A second,' he says roughly, and closes the door. The whisky priest has been redeemed, his weakness turned to glory. He has made the hardest ethical decision of his life and triumphed.

In the end we are pushed back to existentialism and situation ethics. We have to meet each situation as it comes and thrash out our own response. The alternative is to hand our conscience over to the church, or to a guru or a set of Biblical rules and injunctions. That is to lose our personality and to throw away our integrity.

In the last war the SS *Dorchester* was sinking. Four priests – a Methodist, a rabbi, a Roman Catholic priest and a minister of the Reformed Church – stood on deck handing out lifebelts. When they ran out, each of them took off their own safety harness and handed it to another sailor. Then they joined hands and prayed as they went down with the ship.

May God look down in mercy as we struggle to make our choices in this confusing, difficult world.

Hold us tight, Lord, so that we do not spin off into the empty spaces of loneliness.

35

Fear

1 John 4.18
Perfect love casts out fear

Fear was in the air, thick as molasses. This was the rampaging polio outbreak of the late 1940s. I was 12 years old, at boarding school. Most boys had been sent home, but a small group of us had parents who left us to battle it out. The horror of spending our childhood trapped in an iron lung, paralysed, haunted us daily. When my best friend caught the disease, I felt sick. But I was one of the lucky ones and completed my schooldays unafflicted. Looking back, I believe that I had a vague idea of protective angels surrounding us and of God's mercy in the wings.

Émile Zola's novel *Germinal* ends in unbridled horror. It is set in Montsou, a forbidding coal-mining town in a bleak region of northern France. Étienne, a hard-working idealist, gets a job at the pit and falls in love with Catherine, a mere child, employed as a cart-pusher in the depths of the mine. Her master is a vicious brute called Chaval. Étienne engineers a strike, but after a while it fails and the men return to work. Then tragedy overtakes the pit. A revolutionary anarchist blows up the mine, trapping the miners underground and Chaval, Catherine and Étienne in a tiny cavern. The reader needs a strong stomach to continue.

In the ensuing flood, disembowelled horses scream and the abandoned, wretched mineworkers yell with terror. A great fall of rock separates the three from the rest. Catherine weeps as the horse gives its death-rattle. 'Oh my God. Take me away. I'm afraid. I don't want to die.'

Chaval has a little food, but he refuses to share it until Catherine submits to him sexually. When he attempts to rape her, Étienne pulls free a heavy piece of slate and hits him on the head. His body floats in the floodwater where they are trapped. Then the lamp goes out, and they are in eternal night.

In her tortured state, Catherine hears the song of birds, and smells the odour of crushed grass. She sees the sun again and laughs a quiet laugh of love. 'It was at length their wedding night at the bottom of this tomb. They loved each other in despair of everything, in death.' For two days after, her body lies still. She is dead.

At last the rescuers reach Étienne and he is taken out into the blessed light of day. The one redeeming feature – the only easing of the gloom of that terrible scenario – is the love that the doomed couple finally find, wrapped together. That alone has had the capacity, the impetus to drive away their fear and bring them for a few gilded moments close to Paradise.

Jesus must have known terror when he approached Golgotha and saw the equipment of his death lying on the stark hillside. Nails, a hammer, ropes, a spear, a beaker of vinegar mingled with myrrh, and looming over it the instrument of terror: a towering cross. The despairing cry 'O, my God, why have you forsaken me?' tells of the depths of his darkness. The moment of resignation, the culmination of his life, strangely enough brings with it a momentary peace. 'Father into your hands I commit my spirit.'

There is no recipe to free us from fear, no medicine to whisk it away. It permeates the whole gamut of human life. There is fear of bereavement and loneliness, distress at the thought of death and illness. Further down the scale comes worry over an exam or a job interview. Teenagers fear not meeting a partner, and parents are scared when their children take out a car at night for the first time. Yes, it is all there, and it is part of the inexorability of existence.

In St John's gospel are the familiar words 'Perfect love casts out fear'. And therein lies the beginning of an answer. If we can resign ourselves into God's love and feel the air around us vibrating with his presence, then the intensity of fear is lessened.

At times when our lives are fraught, the hand of God seems far away, uninterested, uninvolved. The poet Rilke shows us that, even through the long night, God is close by.

> As it happens, the wall between us
> is very thin. Why couldn't a cry
> from one of us
> break it down? It would crumble
> easily,
> it would barely make a sound.

Crumble the walls that lie between us and God, and our fears are drawn of their poison and our worries resolved into what is bearable. God's love is resilient enough to carry us through thick and thin.

Calm our fears, Lord, and touch us with the richness of your compassion. Amen.

36

Process

Colossians 3.1
Christ is all and in all

It is one of the iconic images of the 1980s. On New Year's Eve 1982, 44 women used ladders to scale the so-called impregnable defences at Aldermaston. At dawn they climbed onto one of the silos containing a nuclear bomb. The picture of them in black-and-white shows their outline silhouetted against the awakening sunrise. Barbed-wire fencing intrudes as they stand on top of something so powerful, so sinister, that it could annihilate London. The image sears itself into the imagination.

Such potentially destructive weapons are evil. One day I visited the site and talked with the women. Lorries rumbled in, forced to stop in front of rows of prone bodies. Police knocked down makeshift tents, and on one occasion women joined hands round the entire length of the perimeter fence. It was a fight against darkness.

Charles Williams – one of the Oxford literary group known as The Inklings, whose members also included C. S. Lewis and J. R. R. Tolkien – codified evil in his dense, complex novel *War in Heaven*. The Holy Grail has been discovered in the country parish of Archdeacon Julian Davenport. Gregory Persimmons, a manipulator of the black arts, steals the chalice and uses it for a Black Mass and as a means of spiritually dominating his rivals. He also has a dark plan to ravish a child's soul, an act of pure evil.

The grail suffers a metaphysical attack, warded off by the intense prayer of the saintly Archdeacon. Persimmons and his satanists try to lure the Archdeacon into their lair and attempt to bind his body to a dead man's soul. It fails because the power of God sets the priest free. Persimmons is arrested, the child is safe, and the Archdeacon dies a holy death on the altar steps during the celebration of the Mass.

The book resurrects the ancient theme of good versus evil and raises an often asked question, How can God allow evil? Why is his once pristine creation splattered with blood? To get round this apparently intractable difficulty we have to reorientate our perception of God completely. He is not an outsider waving a magic wand and enchanting the world into evil. He is written into the very heart of existence, whether it be evil or good.

The thinking lying behind this apparently outrageous claim is called 'process theology'. It begins with the assumption that life is an onward-going process in which the whole universe is involved.

In 1907 the French philosopher Henri Bergson wrote a book called *Creative Evolution*. In it he posited the idea of a life force, an *élan vital*, running throughout creation, gradually drawing it onwards and upwards towards a greater consciousness and complexity. This force is spontaneous, pushing ahead to an unknown future.

Pierre Teilhard de Chardin, the French Jesuit priest, gave this theory a spiritual twist. The evolution of the world has an added ingredient: it is infused with the divine. Through a combination of human and divine love, this ongoing process will reach ever higher and will come to its finality at what he called the 'omega point'. This Christ-fired momentum is a christogenesis that will culminate in God and Christ. He makes an important distinction: God is not all that is – He is *in* all that is.

That throws an entirely different light on evil. Take a barbarity such as modern slavery. It cannot be equated with God, but he is the co-sharer, the joint-sufferer with those being exploited.

It does not stop there. He is also inherent in, although separate from, the very wrongdoing of the traders. It is like adding sugar to tea. The two are separate ingredients, yet they infuse into one in the cup, which represents the world. It follows that every situation, no matter how harrowing, contains divine essence and has the potential to grow into something richer. This can give hope to a world that is sickened by violence.

Jean Pierre de Caussade, a Jesuit and spiritual master, calls on us to dive into the present moment, to search the onward-going process for glimpses of God. The riches uncovered will be infinite. 'The divine will is a deep abyss of which the present moment is the entrance. If you plunge into this abyss you will find it infinitely more vast than your desires.' Never forget that each minute, every hour, all good deeds and evildoing alike are ripe with the presence of Christ.

O God, invisible, unknowable, open our eyes to the divine love woven into the universe. Amen.

37

Music

Revelation 18.22
*The music of harpists and musicians,
pipers and trumpeters*

A sorry downfall awaited the once great city of Babylon; the vision of doom spares nobody. Because of its wrongdoing, it will be thrown down with violence. Light will be snatched from it, and the voices of bride and bridegroom will never again be heard. The final penalty for the wilting city is the death of music: harps, flutes, trumpets and minstrels are silenced for ever. It is a great deprivation. Music is a divine gift, and it has the potential to awaken us to an ecstasy that lies close to prayerfulness.

I was in Ripon Cathedral one lunchtime. The organist, way up above the aisle, was practising. Sweeping waves of sound, glorious, discordant, triumphant and thunderous, rang out over the cathedral. When he had finished, I called out to him, 'What was that piece?' Back came the reply:

Herbert Howells. His voluntary, *Paean*. The music had been a prayer, a melody that had drawn me into the presence of God.

Music can also heal, as Herbert Howells's *Hymn of Paradise* shows, with its eloquence, its haunting beauty, its sense of loss and its final resting in peace. The work lay hidden for a decade until it came to the notice of Vaughan Williams. He insisted that it be performed, even though it had been written as a private composition.

Herbert Howells's only son, Michael, had died, aged ten, in 1935, and his father's grief was so overwhelming that he could not write a single note of music. His daughter suggested that composing might be a way of easing the pain, and so he composed the *Hymn of Paradise*. 'Music may have the power beyond any other medium to offer relief and comfort,' he said. The music starts off troubled and full of anguish; sorrow-laden chords proliferate. When the finale is reached, with the words 'Holy is the true light and passing wonderful', coupled with the promise that Christ's home is one of unfading splendour, the music changes. There is a mystical, limpid quality to it, a beauty lying just beyond our grasp. It sings aloud that Michael, his son, is safely at rest, and the composer himself has found peace.

I recall many musical moments that have revealed for me the elusive nature of God. One was high summer in Italy: a stifling evening at the Baths of Caracalla in Rome. Sitting in the seats the Ancient Romans had occupied so long ago, we listened, awed, to a production of *Aida*. Real camels strolled across the stage, and above us was the velvet Mediterranean night. It was exhilarating, and so moving when, in the closing moments, Radames is buried alive in a deep tomb with his lover, Aida, that the whole of Roman society seemed to weep with them. Music can remind us of God's compassion and love.

On occasion it brings illumination where there is darkness. Part of Henryk Górecki's Third Symphony is written to commemorate the 18-year-old girl Helena, who was incarcerated in a Gestapo cell in Zakopane. The words hurt with their simplicity and plaintiveness as she asks the Blessed Mother for her prayers: 'Mother, no, do not cry. Queen of Heaven most chaste, help me always. Hail Mary.' Whenever I listen to it, I am drawn to utter a silent prayer for all who are imprisoned without hope and subjected to unspeakable cruelty. Mary was there with Helena in the cell, and God too knew of its terrors.

In his Fifth Symphony, Shostakovich reaches a conclusion that resounds with hope. In trouble with the Soviet authorities for writing music that was not pro-Russian, he composed this work which, on the face of it, applauds communism. In fact, it is probably a sideways kick at it. The finale builds up to an unbearable confusion of chords, a cacophony of sound, and then bursts into a triumphant major key for the last few bars.

The message is sublime. The brutality and emptiness of the Stalinist regime will end, and with that news comes a great cry of triumph. Translate that into spiritual terminology, and it is saying that light will always survive and that God's grandeur can never be erased by human wickedness.

All music is prayer in the making, whether it be Olivier Messiaen's spirit-soaked *La Nativité du Seigneur* or Will Todd's ebullient jazz Mass, which turns the creed into a crescendo of passion and sounds forth the Gloria with verve and excitement.

If prayer seems dead and God absent, listen to the music of your choosing. Out of it will come sparks of breathless holiness. Give it a fling and you will find your reward.

Be with us, Lord, through the discordant music of life, and lead us to the harmony of your presence. Amen.

38

Discipline

2 Thessalonians 3.14
*If any man refuses to obey what we
say in this letter, note that man and have
nothing to do with him*

It was 1955. A buff envelope came through the letter-box. My heart sank. I knew what it was: call-up papers for National Service. I reported to Willems Barracks in Aldershot, joined the militia as a private soldier and embarked on one of the most extraordinary voyages of my career. I had never been addressed by a number before, nor had I eaten breakfast out of a battered tin pan while doubling round the parade ground accompanied by the coarse shouts of a sergeant.

The aim of the ensuing two years was simple enough: it was to instil in me instant obedience and teach me unquestioning discipline. Activities would often have been degrading, had we not seen the absurdity of them. I cleaned 176 lavatories during a flu outbreak that felled most of the camp, washed up vast dixies that had been left full of meat that had gone rotten. We picked up from the parade ground pieces of gravel that were not of regulation size, and when we had done that, the sergeant scattered them again and the process was repeated.

Having had my fill of discipline after a boarding-school upbringing and military service, my wife and I decided to bring up our children in such a way that they were not subject to prescriptive rules. They were allowed more than a degree of freedom, and we tried to rear them in an atmosphere of love and kindness. At times they ran rather wild, but the system worked. The proof of the pudding was in the eating, and the evening when both the teenage boys told us that they could not have had better or more caring parents was one of the most moving moments of my life and meant worlds to me.

This needs a degree of clarification. I am not against all discipline: that would lead to worldwide anarchy. But I am antagonistic to that which is imposed on the individual from the outside. Such discipline leaches away freedom and sets up a veiled hostility between the discipline-imposer and the person subjected to the stricture. It goes without saying that the laws of the land must be obeyed, but that is pragmatism rather than morality and carries with it a high degree of self-interest. We obey not least because that ensures that we do not languish behind bars with a police record.

I am thinking rather of another kind of discipline, and its starting-point is our inner being. This discipline is not imposed but is something that we thresh out existentially over the years, and it is bound up with motivation. If we refrain from stealing whisky out of the supermarket because we do not want to take advantage of the shareholders, the staff and the girls on the till, we are imbuing our motivation with what scripture rather ponderously refers to as righteousness.

There is another caveat in this. By advocating freedom of choice I am not suggesting we should have *carte blanche* to ride roughshod over anyone who blocks our path. That is to take a liberty, not to exercise freedom, and in so doing we are depriving another person of their own freedom.

If you are extremely wealthy and live next door to a hospice and decide to build a swimming-pool without regard for all the concomitant noise, inconvenience, traffic and upheaval that may cause, your actions are libertarian and thoroughly selfish. As followers of Christ we are given the blessing of free choice, but there is a rider attached to it. If we do not take on board compassion, thoughtfulness and unselfishness we are veering away from the God of love.

When it comes to the church, a good deal of reshuffling is necessary. No sermon should be draconian, telling us how we should conduct our lives. Nor should we be bound by scriptural dogma or doctrine, for the bottom line is that they are all human constructs, even though perhaps touched by the divine hand. Our world is very different from that in which Christ lived and, unless doctrine and theology are continuously developing to take account of the uncertainty that prevails in the world, we will stagnate intellectually.

The trouble is that it is far easier to take on board an established theological system than to work out our own. Designing a personal one is unnerving, yet at the same time exhilarating. We need to be the captain of our own ship, working out the voyage, searching for significant landmarks and sailing for new seas; and that is a great responsibility.

Mechthild of Magdeburg beautifully expresses the Christ-filled pilgrimage. She can find no happiness, nor can she dance unless the Lord leads her. If he does that, she can 'leap into Love and from Love into Knowledge. And from Knowledge into the harvest, that sweetest fruit beyond human sense.' Once there, she can whirl in a dance with God. And we can join in.

Spin with us, Christ, in the dance of life and guide us surely along the crowded paths. Amen.

39

Darkness and Light

John 1
The light shines in the darkness

It was Christmas Eve on the North Yorkshire Moors. The night was bitter, with driving snow and ice spicules in the air. The car was so cold that my fingers stuck to the door. My boots crunched as I walked between the shadowed tombstones and startled sheep, heading for the church.

Somebody had turned the heating on full blast, for the air was torrid. Sounds came to my ears. The ticking of the church clock, the creaking of the door as the oak settled and the insistent chug of the boiler. But this was something different: a sighing, a soughing of breath. Was it the flutter of angels' wings high up in the rafters? Then I found her, hiding under one of the front pews: 22 years old, shivering, filthy, with fear written over her features. She backed away like a startled roe deer, eyes wide with fright, and I sat down next to her and took her hand as my soutane flowed round me, black in the dim light of the church. I told her I was a priest, showed her my dog collar and promised her I would not hurt her.

Slowly, between tears, the dreadful story poured out. She was terrified of men. She had been raped in a children's home, booted by the police and thrown out. Desperate for shelter from the snow, she had dossed down in a barn, but a farmer saw her off with his dogs. She lay down in a shuttered shop doorway, but she felt threatened and found refuge in the church. Turning up the heating, she hid, longing for sanctuary.

I took her home and asked my wife to give her a bath, and discreetly to take from her the six-inch-bladed knife. She lived with us, a sweet companion, until we found her a home in the Camphill Village.

That night I listened to the reading of the first chapter of St John's gospel, and the words were like pearls in the candlelit church with its faint smell of incense and wax. The reader brought home to me the message so strongly that, apart from my nine years in the desolation of atheism, I have never wavered to this day. The light shines in the darkness, and the darkness has not – and never can – overcome it.

I drew our young woman into my prayers, and tried to envelop her with love and leave the rest to God.

John Taylor, the one-time Bishop of Winchester, tells of an incident when he was working in London in the very early days of Commonwealth immigration. A West Indian woman was told that her husband had been killed in a street accident. Grief shrouded her, and a desperate cloak of misery made her sink deep into a corner of the sofa, unhearing, unseeing. Family and friends could not draw her out of her trance of grief.

Then an English woman who was teaching her children at the local school came and sat beside her. No words were spoken, but she put her arm around the unmoving shoulders, holding them. Her cheek lay against the sufferer's and, as the pain seeped through into the comforter, the bereft wife began to cry, her tears falling on the linked hands of the two women. Still no word was spoken. Then the teacher got up and left in silence.

Her embrace was the hug of God, her kiss the divine mercy. The tense muscles and film of sweat on the mother's brow were the pain of God. That day, light triumphed over darkness, as it always has and always will.

I have seen this same triumph of light in the high-dependency unit of the hospital where I had my cancer operation. The dedication of the cleaners, the efforts of the catering staff to find something that would tempt my appetite, spoke of God's love. The nurses offering comfort and skill, the doctors, consultants and surgeons doing the best for their patients, were divine compassion at work. The chaplains weaving between beds with words of comfort and sacramental sustenance spoke of the healing power of Christ, and sometimes it felt as if the building was watched over by angels. Light shone out over the darkness of pain, suffering and possible death; and I thought again of the invincibility and all-embracing love of Christ.

Gerard Manley Hopkins speaks of this incalculable gift that God has given to his waiting world in his poem 'God's Grandeur'. It will shine out over the world with all the brilliance of a shaken piece of foil, and no matter how man 'sears, blears and smudges' God's blessed handiwork, nature is never ultimately ruined because the dearest, freshest, deep-down things of light live on.

The last four lines lift me into the presence of The Almighty: 'And though the last light off the black West went/Oh, morning, at the brown brink eastward springs.' And why? It is because the Holy Ghost broods over the distorted world 'with warm breast and with ah! bright wings'. As I face the closing days of my life, that is all I need to know.

Lord, your light is inextinguishable, brighter by far than a thousand suns. Warm us, if you will, in your rays. Amen.

40

Resurrection

Matthew 28.7
Tell his disciples that he has risen from the dead

Traditionally on Easter Day we fill the pews and listen with growing wonder and perhaps a touch of the disciples' disbelief as the timeless narrative evolves. There is the empty tomb in the dawn half-light, the scurrying women, the angel in white and the other disciples, who did not know whether to be joy-filled or scared out of their minds.

We hear again the familiar story of Mary mistaking Jesus for the gardener, and we tread wearily along the Emmaus road with the disciples as they slowly realize the identity of their companion. Thomas's bragging doubt and the amazing catch of fish add yet more zing to the drama.

And that is precisely what it is: a drama, and we are the audience. That is the weakness. For Easter to flower in all its glory, we have to do some drastic theological reshaping. We need to re-evaluate our role in the myth. We are not lookers-on from the wings. Easter calls on us to join the cast and take an active part, rather than lurking behind the safety curtains.

Gerard Manley Hopkins's poem 'The Wreck of the *Deutschland*' takes a bold theological side-step and reinvents the Easter drama. It was Saturday 7 December 1875, and the steamship *Deutschland* out of Bremen lay 20 miles off Harwich, bound for New York. On board were 70 crew members and 123 emigrants heading for a new life in America. Accompanying them were five nuns exiled from Germany under anti-Catholic laws.

There is a grinding of metal, a shuddering, violent shock as the ship strikes a submerged sandbank, the Kentish Knock. She lies there helpless, her back broken, smashed by waves. A brave sailor climbs the mast in a vain attempt to rescue a child. Crew members struggle to get passengers into the rigging away from the waves. 'Night roared, with the heart-break hearing a heart-broke rabble, / The woman's wailing, the crying of child without check.' For Hopkins, this is a replaying of Christ's passion; and there is malevolent darkness over land and sea. The ship has become the cross. For all on board, it is Good Friday.

Then something unexpected and profoundly moving occurs. One of the coiffed nuns, tall, gaunt, blinded by sea-drift, staggers to the middle of the deck. Her words ride out over the storm's incessant howling: 'Oh Christ, Christ, come quickly.' Her shout is drowned in engulfing water as she is swept away. Here the poet takes over and, in a passionate outpouring, asks the dead nun, now in heaven, to pray for the entire English nation and the shipwrecked voyagers. Then he pleads with the Lord to return in all his glory. 'Let him easter in us, be a Dayspring in the dimness of us, be a crimson-cresseted east.' The whole thrust of the poem has changed from despair to hope. Christ is envisioned as 'master of the tides', the snow turns to lilies, and flowers and heaven lie beyond the dark, stormy night.

Now comes the punchline. To fathom the true meaning of Easter we need a decisive, attention-seizing verb: 'to easter'. Easter is not just a drama acted on the bare slopes of Calvary, climaxing at the empty tomb. It is not a series of events to be observed, quantified, thought over, questioned and discussed. Nor is it a riveting tale with a happy ending. It has far richer connotations. It is something that has to seize us and overpower us. We need to be 'eastered'. 'To easter' has a nautical ring. It means to steer a ship to the light of the dawning day, so that it is flooded with the rays of the rising sun.

Easter is the starting-point for an inner transformation of our being. All our desolation, despair, fear, hate, wrongdoing and uncertainty are encompassed by the light of the risen Christ and transformed into a rich patina of what is fruitful, joyous and constructive. It is an overwhelming event that reshapes our destiny, reorienting our spiritual path and lifting us up into the presence of God.

Thou mastering me
God! Giver of breath and bread;
World's strand, sway of the sea;
Lord of living and dead

No wonder we emerge from the church on Easter morning with burgeoning joy, our vision sharpened, our compassion rekindled, prayer enriched and thanksgiving renewed.

The principle of love woven into the universe has prevailed not only over the wreck of the *Deutschland* but over the whole waiting world. Christ the 'Pride, rose, prince, hero of us, high-priest' has brightened the dark universe and eastered in us. This is the blessed vision that I hope will be with me until I breathe my last. Praise be to the God whose love surpasses all knowing.

From the day of our birth, Lord Jesus Christ, you have been with us in this uncertain world. Of your mercy, remain with us at and beyond our ending. Amen.

ACKNOWLEDGEMENTS

I would like to thank the team at Bloomsbury Publishing for their encouragement and enthusiasm and my wife, Victoria, for her unfailing love and support during difficult times.

PERMISSIONS